The Men That Stole My Soul

KELiCHiA

www.TalentedAuthoress.com

First published November 2007

KELiCHiA

INTRODUCTION

I don't know what it is that has gotten me started with telling people about my life, but I thought that it was about time someone heard what I have to say. Maybe it was my reading the life story of Karrine Steffans. Maybe it was my reading about 2004 American Idol, Fantasia and her life trials and tribulations. Whatever it is, I am glad I finally decided to do so. Life is easy for some people, and it is hard for others. No matter what may happen in your life, whether good or bad, it is up to you to maintain what you have or change what you have for the better. I wish that I could tell you every single detail about my life in this one book, but there is not enough paper in the world for that. I just wanted to give those that are close to me an idea of where my attitude comes into play. I wanted to give them the reason why I act the way that I do towards some people and the reason why I seem so shut out to the world around me. The series of events that are stated in this story happens over a period of nine years. That may seem like a very long time to some, but to me it seems like yesterday. I am so happy that I am learning to cope with the things that have happened in my life. I am still working on forgiving those events that have happened to me. I am writing this story to somehow bring closure to the chapters of my life, so that I may move on. I am not going to dwell on my childhood too much. Sometimes, it is what happens in your adulthood that changes your perspective on life. In this book, I will hit on a few things about my childhood that I have never told a soul.

KELiCHiA

CHAPTER ONE- THE MEETING

I am a single mother of two sons and a Sergeant in the United States Army. It is December 2005, I am currently in Baghdad, Iraq, and I am awaiting our departure from here to the states. I have been here for twelve months, now. It was a step of faith and fighting my pride on my joining the military. I was down and out with nothing to show for all of the things I had accomplished at an early age. One of my accomplishments is that I am a licensed cosmetologist, going on nine years. Wow. That feels good to say. I earned my cosmetology license, while I was in high school, in 1997. I was seventeen years old. I attended what some of you might know as VOTECH. That is vocational technical school. I was always good at setting high goals and achieving them. That may have been hard for many others, but not hard for Twinky. Twinky is my nickname, since birth. Shortly after I graduated high school, I turned 18. August 1997 is when I earned my certificate for nursing assistant.

So, there you have it, an eighteen year old with two careers to fall back on. I had also moved into my first home. My first official home was a single-wide trailer. I loved it. It seems like I had it going on. Right? Wrong. Oh, don't get it twisted. Things were going great. They were going great, until I met my children's father. For disclosure purposes, I will just call him Zic. I first met Zic at one of the three jobs that I had. Oh yeah, I didn't mention that I obtained a third job after I earned my nursing assistant certificate. Aside from working in my mother's salon and in a nursing home, I also worked as a server at a well-known late night diner. I was living it up. Anyway, as I was explaining, my third job was where I met Zic. To me, he was fine. He was very attractive. Anyone who goes to any of these late night eat-in diners should be familiar with the quarter machines that have the stuffed animals in them. I would spend my spare time winning and collecting stuffed animals out of the machine that was in the restaurant. I was good at catching the animals with the *claws of life*, on the first try. One particular stuffed animal always seemed difficult for me to catch. I simply gave up on winning this stuffed animal after so many tries and no victories. I will never forget this animal. It was a teddy bear dressed up in a Yankee's baseball outfit. I just had to have him for my collection. One night, I was tending to the salad bar and cleaning its surrounding areas, when I noticed this guy coming in for a pick-up order. I glanced at him and kept on doing what I was doing. Upon my noticing him about to leave, I just could not resist telling him that I thought that he was cute. After my compliment, I kept on cleaning and straightening up. All the while, I never once noticed that he was at the stuffed animal machine. Suddenly, I was interrupted by a "*psst*" sound. When I looked up, Zic handed me a teddy bear. You guessed it. It was the Yankee bear. I smiled as I took the bear from him. The line that came next was the line that made me even more attracted to this man.

He handed me the bear and said, "I left a number on it and you can use it if you want to."

Upon the completion of his line, Zic left the restaurant, leaving me speechless. I couldn't believe it. He left me standing there, mesmerized. He hadn't left me feeling repulsed by him. As the night went on, I could not get Zic off my mind. I didn't waste any time calling Zic. We talked a little bit and told each other a bit about one another. We talked for a couple of hours. Before hanging up, Zic offered to take me out on a date. I told him I would think about it and get back to him. At that point in my life, I thought that I had it great. I was single, I had three jobs, I had my own place, and that guy could be the one. I don't know what it was about him, and to this day, I still don't know what attracted me to him. It could have been the dumb line that he threw at me, or maybe it was the way he seemed like a gentleman. He didn't pressure me for anything. A couple of weeks of working and talking to Zic went by. One night, I came into the diner to work and found out that I was not on the schedule for the night. I didn't want it to seem like I had wasted my time by driving for *twenty* minutes to come to work, only to turn around and go right back home. Besides, I didn't have a car of my own and was borrowing my mother's car at the time. I didn't feel like returning the car right away. I did what any young woman, in my situation, would have done. I called Zic to see if he had anything planned for the night. I informed him that I didn't have to work for the night. We both agreed to go out somewhere to hang out. Zic drove to the diner to meet me, and he insisted that he would drive. I left the diner with him in his blue Escort. The first place that he and I went to was another diner that was down the street from where I worked. . While waiting for the waitress, Zic and I made jokes about a lot of things and laughed. We actually had a blast. The waitress finally arrived to take our orders. She had a really nasty attitude.

That was not cool. Zic loudly said what I was thinking, "That's one dollar from her tip!"

We both laughed so loud, that we got a little unwanted attention from the other patrons. We ate our meal and prepared to leave. Upon leaving, Zic poured his glass of orange juice and all of the syrups onto the table, and we ran out of the diner—after paying, of course. After we gathered ourselves from laughing so hard, Zic told me that he was having a good time. I told him the same. We didn't want the night to end. We decided to go somewhere else, and I let him choose. We drove to the nearest gas station and filled up the tank. Before I knew it, we were on our way. After about an hour and a half of driving, we ended up in Virginia Beach. At that time, it was around *midnight*. I worked the night shift at the diner, which was perfect for our nighttime rendezvous. While we were on the way to Virginia Beach, Zic asked me something that was definitely not on my *perfect man for me résumé*.

He asked me, "Do you mind if I smoke a cigarette?"

This is the moment, in the movies, where the stranger walks into the saloon and you would hear the record scratch and stop playing. I couldn't believe it. This fool asked me did I mind if he smoked a cigarette. We had gone too far at this point. I was really starting to like this fool.

So being the naïve and crazy, young-minded girl that I was, I told him, "No, I don't mind."

I knew damn well that I was lying through my teeth. Being the non-smoker that I was, I had a good nose for cigarette smokers. He must have been good at hiding the scent, because I never smelled it on him. Damn. That was strike one, on my hit list, that I let slide. In order to cover my mishap on his first offense, I asked him if he had his high school diploma.

His response was, "No. I dropped out of high school, but I went back to get my GED."

My immediate self-thought was, *cool*, at least he has his GED. We finally arrived at Virginia Beach and found a parking space. We got out of the car, and I told him that I had to use the restroom or it wasn't going to be a pretty sight. All of the businesses were closed due to it being late at night. We went to every hotel, and there weren't any clerks to be found. We finally arrived at one hotel, with a clerk that was visible.

I kindly yelled to the person behind the thick glass, "Could I please use the restroom?"

The person shook his head, no. I was devastated. Zic asked me if I had gone to the restroom. I told him, "no."

He went up to the thick window that the clerk was standing behind, and he banged on the window. He began yelling at him to allow me to use the restroom. I guess the clerk was startled and scared. The clerk decided to give Zic the key to let me into the restroom. Boy, was that a relief. After I relieved myself, Zic and I walked alongside the waves of the ocean. My inexperience led me to believe that we were having a romantic time. I lived a strict and sheltered life growing up. Zic and I sat on an empty bench and conversed for a bit. I was cold with the thin jacket that I had on. Zic was a gentleman and gave me the jacket that he had on. I laid my head on his lap, while we talked, laughed, and joked about everything. A couple of hours had quickly gone by, and we decided to return home. After all, I wanted our arrival time to match up with my shift's hours, so that my mother wouldn't become enraged at me for keeping her vehicle too long. Don't get me wrong. I love my mother, dearly, but I knew she kind of had issues back then. You'll find out a little later on what I meant by that comment. Over the next couple of weeks, Zic and I were constantly talking to each other. I thought that it was great. I didn't realize that I was slowly not giving a damn what was going on around me, because I was *occupied*.

KELiCHiA

CHAPTER TWO-THE BEGINNING OF THE DOWNSLIDE

I know that it is hard for most females to do it, but if at all possible, listen to your mother. There are so many times that I wish I had listened and taken heed to what my mother was telling me for my own good. Here I am thinking that talking to this Zic character was something that was meant to be. My mother had become suspicious that I was seeing someone. One day, she decided to satisfy her curiosity's hunger. She asked me about the guy that I was seeing and talking to so much. I told her who he was and where he was from. She surprised me by saying that I needed to leave him alone. She also stated to me that she knew some people from the area that Zic was from that could possibly be related to him. She told me that if they were related, their family was no good. Most females would go by what their mother tells them. Not me. Not Twinky. It was just another opening for me to rebel against my mother's words. I didn't listen and still invited Zic to come to my house. Even though I was living on my own and paying my own bills, I still found myself sneaking Zic into my home. My mother still had her powerful hold on me. She liked to dictate everything that was going on around her. I wasn't any help, because I didn't have enough backbone to stand up to her and tell her to stay out of my life and my business. My mother lived within *five* minutes walking distance from me. Talk about a family affair. There was this time that I skipped out on my day job, which was working at my mother's hair salon. I had made up a story in order to be away from work. Not planning on it, I called Zic. I decided that he should come over, because I didn't have to work. He came over, and he wanted to take me out. I told him that it was okay. I told him to wait while I took a shower. He was watching television in my room. Only *five* minutes had passed when Zic ran into the bathroom and told me that someone was knocking at my front door. I immediately got out of the shower and tried to run and lock the back door, but it was too late. In walks my mother. She saw my naked body and Zic in my room. I can imagine the automatic thought that popped into her mind. Without thought, she began yelling and telling him to get out. She slapped my face hard as hell. She did it right in front of him. Zic left, and I had to listen to my mother's mouth all day. I didn't care though. Rebelling against my mother, I called Zic and told him he could still come over. Zic would knock on the back door, and I would let him in. Do you remember when I said that this was my own home? All that sneaking wasn't cool, but it only seemed to be the right thing to do at the time. On one occasion, I received a knock at the back door. To my surprise, it wasn't Zic. It was a police officer, who immediately started asking me questions like, did I know who Zic was, and why was he sneaking around my home in the dark. I explained to the officer that I knew who Zic was. I also explained to the officer that we had to sneak because my mother didn't want me to have males in my home. The next thing out of the officer's mouth shocked me into my right mind.

He asked, "Whose name is on the lease?"

I told him, "My name is on the lease."

He told me that I needed to tell that to my mother. He also told me to watch the sneaking around, and he left. Frustrated, I took Zic by the jacket and snatched him into the house. We went into my room, which is where I kept my television. I didn't have one in the living room. Thinking back on it, I sure do wish I had put a television in the living room. That would have saved me from a lot of heartache and pain. We talked for a while and listened to some music. After about an hour of making out and touching on each other, we took it a little further by taking off our clothes. I wasn't ashamed of my body. In fact, I loved to show my body off every chance that I was afforded. We ended up having intercourse shortly after that. We were protected, of course. Intercourse hurt to an extent. I was not that experienced, and sex was not an everyday thing for me. After Zic and I were finished, we came to the realization that the condom, we were using, had torn. I asked him how he could have not known that the condom had broken.

He responded by saying, "I don't know. All I know is, it felt good and all of a sudden, it got better."

Damn was the first thought that ran across my mind. You see, my mother never really talked about birth control with me. Her idea of birth control was not to have sex at all. Anyway, at that point in time, birth control *should haves* and *could haves* were out of the window. The only thing left to do was to wait and see what was going to happen. I didn't believe in abortions, and giving my baby up for adoption was definitely out of the question. A couple of weeks went by, and the thought of being pregnant had slipped my mind. There was something about me that my mother had noticed. She had noticed that I was always tired. Apparently, mother knows best. In this case, mother did.

She asked me "Do you think you're pregnant?"

My response was, "I don't know."

She told me to go to a doctor and find out. I went to a Women's Clinic the next day. I went into the clinic and filled out some paperwork, paid my *five* dollars, took the cup that the nurse had given me, and went into the bathroom. The nurse, that was there, told me to hand her the cup as soon as I was finished. I stuck my hand out of the bathroom door and handed the cup of urine to the nurse. I washed my hands and stepped out of the bathroom. The moment that I stepped out of the bathroom, the nurse handed me a piece of paper. I thought to myself, *what now?* I looked at the paper, and the word *POSITIVE* was written on the paper. My heart dropped about ten inches. On the other hand, I was kind of excited.

The nurse asked me, "What do you want to do?"

I looked at her, like she was an alien.

I told her, plain and simple, "I'm going to keep it."

The nurse smiled and wished me luck. I went to my mother's house to tell her the results. When I arrived at my mother's house, I took a deep breath, got out of the car, and entered the house. The house was quiet. I went into my mother's room, where she was asleep.

I called her name, "Mama."

She woke up. My mother's very nosy. That's why it only took me calling her once, in order for her to wake up.

The first thing out of her mouth was, "What'd they say?"

I gave her the paper that had the results on it.

She read it and said, "Oh", nonchalantly.

I thought, *Damn. That's it?*

I left and went on about my business. A few hours had passed, and I received a phone call from my mother asking me what the results were. Now, I could have sworn that I went by her house earlier and told her. I told her that I told her what the results were, earlier. She asked me what they were, again.

I told her, "POSITIVE."

"Umph, umph, umph", was her response.

We hung up with each other, and I called Zic to tell him the news. He took it well. From there, I went on with my life, or so I

thought.

CHAPTER THREE-FOOLISHNESS TAKING ME OVER

Being a fool should be against the law. For the next couple of months, I became Zic's fool. I would do things like pick him up from other females' houses or drop him off at work and sleep in the car and wait until he got off. We would constantly argue, and my body was growing weak and weary. On one of our arguing occasions, Zic had gone out and gotten drunk. I guess he decided that he wanted to come home and pick on me. For what reason? I don't know. All I remember is I started to yell back at him and say my peace. Next thing I know, he'd spit in my face. In shock, I did the only thing that any person in this situation would do. I spit back on him. I should have noticed the signs of his abuse much earlier than I did. Like I stated before, I was a fool. Besides, I was pregnant, and no man wants a woman with a baby. Right? That's the thought that was in my mind. Some days of the pregnancy were miserable. I would try anything to make myself have a miscarriage. I would do things like fall, stomach first, on the floor. I would also cry, all of the time, in order to keep my stress levels high. My life wasn't supposed to turn out that way. I was supposed to be on my way to success, not on my way to being doomed. I prayed and prayed for better days. It had gotten to the point where I wished Zic would die. He was getting on my last damn nerve. There was this one instance where I found a gun in his room. He was hiding it from his nosy ass mother. He was sitting on a chair in his room. I took the gun, walked over to Zic, and I placed the gun against his temple. I asked him if he thought the gun was loaded. He laughed as if I was playing. I pulled the trigger. *Click.* That was the wonderful sound of an empty gun. I had removed the bullets from the gun. Zic didn't see me do that. He was scared to death. It seemed like he was going to piss in his pants. That was so funny, to me, at the time. Days and weeks had passed, and the drama grew stronger. One morning, I had decided that I was fed up and I decided to leave. I got dressed and walked out the door. I had no car. So, I just started walking. Zic shortly realized that I was gone a little too long. He ran down the street looking for me. He was yelling my name very loudly. I just ignored him and kept on walking. He caught up with me, breathing heavily and crying like a baby. I just laughed at how idiotic he looked. After about an hour of his talking my head off and begging and walking, I decided to just go back to the apartment with him. I really didn't have anywhere else to go. The next few months were hell. We would argue, I would cry, and he'd apologize. I had quit all three of my jobs and abandoned my home. The doctors had put me on bed rest. I was diagnosed with preeclampsia (high blood pressure during pregnancy). Because I was bed-ridden, I wasn't allowed to stand for long periods of time. I was so miserable. I could no longer afford to pay all of my bills. Zic's small ass check was nothing.

I gave birth to my first child in June of 1998. After I had given birth, the typical routine of social workers and other authorities visiting the room had begun. The social worker asked me if I knew who the father of my child was.

I happily answered, "Yes."

She told me that the father would have to sign the birth certificate. Zic refused, because he said that he didn't want to get stuck with the hospital bill. What a dumb ass. I was able to go home a couple of days after my child was born. Unfortunately, my child could not go home. He was born prematurely. The doctors wanted to monitor him some more. They wanted to make sure that he could gain weight properly and keep it on. I would walk about five miles to and from the hospital to be with my baby. After about three weeks of hospitalization, my baby was able to come home. The first couple of weeks, of having the baby home, were hectic and depressing for me. Zic would go to work, and I'd be stuck at home with a baby who was very independent. I was a young mother. I didn't know how to handle a little person. There were times when it seemed the baby would cry louder whenever I would pick him up to calm him down. I tried to breast feed him. I didn't get the opportunity to try it in the hospital. He just wouldn't bond with me. I was becoming more and more frustrated with this baby.

He didn't like me. I was suffering from postpartum depression. I would cry, because the baby wouldn't fall asleep on my chest like he did with Zic. I didn't feel needed or wanted by anyone. I felt alone, in spite of having a baby in the house. That was around the time that more abuse had started between me and Zic. One evening, we were in the room, talking. I can't recall what the conversation was about, but it led to us arguing and yelling. The next thing I knew, my head was being slammed against the mirror of the dresser. Then my body was flung across the room, almost tipping over the baby's crib. I couldn't believe it. The *asshole* had put his damn hands on me. I did the natural thing. I slapped and punched the hell out of his face. Eventually, I had gotten evicted and was forced to leave the single-wide trailer that I lived in. All of the arguing and police visits were the last straw for the community that I lived in. I was hurt. I wish I hadn't been so stupid. I was still young, and I had a lot of growing up to do.

KELiCHiA

CHAPTER FOUR-WHY ME

Damn! I'm a teenager, with nowhere to live, and I have a baby. What's a young girl to do? Zic ended up going back to the area that he was from, and he had found himself a place to live. I had to beg him to let us stay with him. He didn't want me on the lease, because it would raise the rent. His dumb ass didn't want to take care of his child. What a deadbeat. We finally moved into the apartment that Zic had gotten. I could tell that reality was hitting him really hard. He did not want to be a father. He realized that he didn't get all of his partying, drinking and hanging out with friends, out of his system. He was not ready for a family. He should have thought about all of that before he unbuttoned his pants. Well, we were living in this new apartment. These were new surroundings for me, and I was bored out of my mind. Not much longer after we had moved in, Zic lost his job, and he had gone on a drastic search to find another one. After all, he did have a family to support. Zic still wanted to go out, party, and hang as if he had the money to do it. Trying to keep up with the Joneses is what I call it. He knew damn well what he was doing. But what can one expect from someone who wasn't that educated. Oh yeah, I forgot to inform you of a conversation that Zic and I had. He had mentioned his not having his GED.

I told him, "I thought you said that you had one."

He said, "I told you that I went to school to get my GED. I never said that I got one."

Damn! This dude was on strike two. About a month went by, and Zic finally got a job at a popular restaurant. His brother was one of the managers there. I didn't have a job, any friends, and was always stuck in the house. I had no social life. The days were growing longer, and I was growing more and more miserable with each day that passed by. I ended up getting pregnant, again. I was getting myself deeper and deeper into a mess. One night, Zic came in late. I was up waiting. He ended up wanting to have sex. I didn't, because I was pregnant and miserable. All I remember is we ended up arguing, and he carried me down the stairs and outside to try and lock me out of the house, barefoot and all. I ran back to the front door as fast as I could. I pushed the door for it to open as he tried to push the door to close it. The neighbors banged on the wall for us to stop the noise. Next thing I knew, things were being thrown around and broken all over the place. I remember ending up next door, at the neighbor's apartment. I was greeted by the officers at the neighbor's apartment. It took me a while to notice that I was bleeding all over their carpet, from my left foot. I had stepped on some of the broken glass that was in our apartment, and I didn't pay much attention when I did it. The officer asked me if I needed an ambulance.

I told him, "No."

He proceeded to tell me the consequences of a domestic dispute.

I told him, "It will never happen again."

KELiCHiA

I knew that I did not want to go to jail. I had a little common sense, believe it or not. Time had passed, and more arguing went on. I was pregnant for a second time. I just kept getting deeper and deeper into that horrific lifestyle. On a daily basis, I would ask myself, *what did I do to deserve what is happening to me?* I remember, one time, I had called my mother to come and pick me up. I was tired of Zic's abuse. I didn't have a car, but I had somehow found a way to the restaurant that I used to work at. I wanted to get away as soon and as quickly as possible. My mother met me at the restaurant that I told her I would be at. I should have known better than to call her, anyway. Something just didn't seem right. We talked for a few minutes. I had told her about Zic's abuse and the things that he'd said and done to me.

She said, "Maybe y'all need to talk to each other."

I was in shock. No, she didn't just tell me that we needed to talk. She ended up driving me back to the apartment. She basically told me that the kids and I couldn't stay with her, because we weren't on her lease. How scandalous was that? This takes me back to when I was pregnant with my first child. My mother and I were sitting in her room one day, and I decided to share something with her that I had never shared with anyone else. I thought I was telling her this particular bit of information, woman to woman. I told about an instance that happened when I was twelve. She had a boyfriend named T. T was in his early twenties and my mother was in her early thirties. One night, I had come out of the bathroom. I had just taken a shower, and I closed my room door. I took my towel off, so that I could get dressed for bed. At that same instance, T had opened my bedroom door. Even though he had apologized, he stood there, for what seemed like an eternity and stared at me. I ran to the door, as quickly as I could, and told him to get out. I slammed the door in his face. Another moment was when I was getting into the back seat of the car. I was almost in the car when I felt a hand slide across my butt. I turned and gave him the evil eye.

The pervert said, "It is so pretty."

After all of that was said and done, my mother had the

audacity to say, "Well, what did you do to provoke him to do that?"

What a BITCH! What kind of mother would say some shit like that? I was in disbelief of what she had said to me. My frame of mind was beginning to change, slowly but surely. There I was, eighteen and pregnant, and I had no motherly support. Damn. I was pretty much back in the same boat with this woman. I couldn't trust her as far as I could throw things on her. She took me back to that dude and his abuse. She was only concerned about her stupid lease. She didn't want me and my kids to stay with her, because we weren't on her lease. So much for having an understanding mother. I tried and tried to tell her that I didn't want to be there anymore, but she would not listen. I didn't have anyone to protect me. Here we go. Same old shit, just another day. For breakfast and dinner, this man whooped my ass, or whenever he felt it feasible. No lunch whooping, because he went to work during the day. Thank God for that, because that gave me a break from harm. That was my time for peace. I would do Tae Bo, in my spare time, in order to build my strength. My pregnancy was getting further along, and the beatings were getting worse. One night, Zic and I had gotten into a terrible argument. I can't remember what it was for. All I know is I had gone into the bathroom to do my hair. Suddenly, I felt a lamp being slammed into the side of my stomach. Thank God I didn't turn all the way around, or I may have lost my pregnancy. I picked up the lamp that Zic had slammed into my stomach. I wanted to give him a dose of his own medicine, so I slammed it against his head. I was so tired of the abuse. It had to stop. We began fighting and throwing things. My first born was lying on our bed, while the fighting was going on. The fighting and the arguing had gotten heavier and louder. Zic ran into the living room and started breaking all of my furniture. That's right, my furniture! This dude didn't have anything to call his own. He had broken everything of mine that was in his sight. That bastard! I tried my best to stop him, but my body was growing tired from arguing and being pregnant. All of a sudden, Zic ran into the bedroom. My first thought was *oh my God, the baby!* I swore that if that dude did anything to harm my baby, the FEDS wouldn't even be able to identify his

38

dismembered body. I ran after him screaming for him to get out of the room. He took my television, and he threw it on the floor. He took one of his weights, and he dropped it onto the screen of the television. His first attempt didn't work, so the dumb fuck tried again. He shattered the television screen with the weight. I pushed his big ass out of the room and guarded the doorway so that the baby wouldn't get hurt. In the midst of all the chaos, we didn't hear the neighbors, that were next door and underneath us, banging on the ceiling and the walls for us to quiet down. We also didn't realize that the police were called, and they were knocking at the door. I had gone downstairs to answer the door and let the police know what was going on. They asked to come in, and I let them in. They saw the mess that had been rendered throughout the house. When they realized that an infant was around, they told us that social services was going to be contacted. My heart immediately dropped and started throbbing. I was now at risk for having my son taken away from me. I wasn't showing too much, so I didn't mentioned that I was pregnant. The police made Zic leave the apartment in order for us not to go to jail. The police instructed me not to let him back in or there would be consequences for the both of us and our son would, in fact, be taken. I was so hurt and the night was getting later and later. What the hell had just happened? All of this in one blink of an eye. In the middle of my early morning sobbing, I heard a light knock at the front door. I wiped my tears and went downstairs to answer. It was Zic. He asked me to please open the door he needed to talk to me. My dumb brainwashed ass opened the door and let the punk in. Then came the *sorries* and *please forgive mes* and the *it'll never happen agains.* I soaked it all in, again.

The next morning, without fail, a Social Services representative had come to the apartment. Little did she know, a couple of hours before she came, Zic and I had cleaned the apartment as best as we could. As she was walking up the stairs, she was looking around to see what mishaps she could find for reporting. After a couple of hours of questioning and evaluation, she explained that this was a child neglect case and it was going to court. I was so devastated. Damn! Damn! Damn! What else could go wrong? Well, let me tell what else went wrong. Zic and I were actually able to pass the time for the awaited court date without fighting and arguing. We were both terrified that our son was going to get taken away. The day came to pass rather quickly. We finally arrived at the courthouse and entered the courtroom. After explaining both sides of our stories and thorough evaluation, the judge decided not to have our child taken away. He ordered us to attend parenting classes for fourteen weeks. On top of that, I was ordered to attend domestic violence classes for sixteen weeks. It was hell. Not the classes themselves, but the way I had to struggle to get there. In order to get to the parenting classes, we had to catch a bus about three miles away from where we lived. The bus didn't turn down the road that led to the school that held the parenting classes. After getting off of the bus, Zic and I had to walk another two miles while pushing our son in a stroller. It was still early in my pregnancy, and I wasn't feeling any sickness. I wasn't showing either. That helped a little bit. The fourteen weeks of parenting classes went by rather quickly. Unfortunately, the domestic violence classes seemed to drag out. Why me?

CHAPTER FIVE-SMOTHERED IN SADNESS

Days had passed, and classes had come and gone. I was full of so much sorrow. My esteem was low to the ground. I walked around with my head hung low, all of the time. I had alienated myself from the world. One day, I told myself that I couldn't live like this. I decided to go out and look for a job. I never wanted to work at a fast food establishment, because I always thought that I was worth much more. After days of searching and tons of applications, I had found a job that suited me the most. It was at a hair salon that wasn't too far from where I lived. I was still early in my second pregnancy, and I wasn't showing. At this point, I didn't tell anyone that I was pregnant. The salon manager liked what she heard and saw, and she decided to hire me. I was pleased. After a few days of catching the bus and working there, the owner had asked if there would be anything that would hinder my building a clientele base.

I decided to come out and tell her, "Yes, there is something that would stop me from working in the future. I'm five months pregnant."

She was very understanding, and she was only concerned about my coming back after the baby was born.

I told her, "I would like to."

We left it at that. About a month of working there had passed, and I was starting to show. No one could tell that I was pregnant, unless I told them. In a way, that was good. It kept my stress levels down. My mom would call the job, every now and again, to check on me. I didn't have a house phone, and that was my only means of communication. One day, my mother had called me. She wanted me to come and visit her. I agreed. I was bored out of my mind doing the same thing, every single day. She came to pick me and my son up, and she took me to her house for a couple of days. One morning, we had gone to my mother's place of business to hang out with her. It was me, my son, and my younger brother. After a few hours of being there, my mother decided that

44

we were bored, and she told me to take myself, my son, and my brother to see our granny. I gladly took her car keys and commenced to driving that forty-five minute drive across the water. It was a beautiful April day. My belly wasn't showing, yet. So, I thought that I was in the clear. I sat in the living room, with my granny, and talked about many things with my grandmother. She had reached out for my son to come and sit in her lap. To our surprise, he actually went to her. That was very weird. He'd never wanted to go near my granny, because when she smiled, she'd have no dentures in. My son, at the time, didn't have any teeth of his own. I guess it was scary for him to see someone that looked the same way that he did. Granny held him for as long as he'd let her. She was happy about him wanting to sit in her lap. Granny enjoyed the company of her first and only great-grandchild, at the time. After a couple of hours of sitting and talking, my grandpa walked down the hallway, into the living room.

He stopped in his tracks, turned to me and said, "You're gaining a little weight. Is there something you wanna tell me?"

I just chuckled at his comment and ignored him.

My granny leaned towards me and whispered, "You can't hide anything from him."

I whispered back to her, "I don't know what I'm going to do with another child."

It wasn't any of grandpa's or anybody else's business.

She then told me, "The child is going to be healthy, and you are going to be alright."

There's nothing on this Earth like Grandmothers. They are the glue that keeps the family together. I love my Granny so much! After a couple more hours of visiting my Grandparents, my brother and I had to leave to give my mother's car back. As we were walking to the car, a funny feeling stung my gut. Something just didn't seem to be sitting right. My Grandparents would always stand at the glass storm door to wave and watch our car as we drove away. That particular time, I looked back to wave at my Granny as she was watching from the door. I saw something in her face. The look in her eyes just wasn't right. I drove off until we couldn't see the house anymore. While I was driving down the road, I told my brother, "I can't wait to get a car of my own, so that I can come and take Granny somewhere."

My Grandfather had purchased a new car, and he always stayed gone. He hardly took my Granny with him, any place. All in all, I still had a gut feeling that something just wasn't right. I just couldn't put my finger on it. I had given my mother her car back. Shortly after, she had closed her salon up and we drove to her house. I couldn't stand being at my mother's house for very long. Her house was so boring and bland. I can't even remember if she had a TV in the house. If she did, she had no cable and no reception. It was pointless being there. Later on that evening, she decided to tell me that she didn't think that it was best for me to go back to Zic. She didn't want me to be stressed and have high blood pressure, like the last pregnancy.

I thought to myself, *this bitch has some nerve trying to be caring, when she's the one that took me back to this dude, when I first tried to leave him.* I had become accustomed to the beatings and the verbal abuse. It had become second nature to me. I had come to the conclusion that, at least, I was getting attention. Like I said before, I was use to the turmoil. Naturally, I started ranting and raving about wanting to go home. She knew that I didn't have a car and any money. I had no other choice but to be there. I was there for a couple of days, and I was about to go crazy. My mother loved having control over me. She could never gather the idea that I was an adult. A few more days had passed, and I was sick of being around her. My mother wanted me to be away from stress, but she was part of all of the problems that I was having. I guess Zic had gotten a little fed up with not having me and the baby in the house. He borrowed his mother's car and came to my mother's house to get us. It may have seemed like I was happy to see Zic, but I was really happy to get the hell away from my mother. She was getting on my last nerve. The way she acted towards me, you'd have thought that she was my child's father. I just wanted out of this life.

KELiCHiA

It was moments like these that made me wish that my childhood attempts at suicide had worked. At the age of twelve, I had it rough. I had a younger brother. My mother used to work me like a slave and treat him like gold. My brother and I are seven years apart. My mother was always at work. She never had time for her family. That stupid hair salon was all she cared about. She was very strict, and she never let me do anything. I had to stay in the yard. I couldn't even go next door to play with my friend. I just stayed cooped up in the house. One afternoon, my mother had called the house and told me to clean up my brother's room. I thought to myself, *what the hell is wrong with his arms and legs?*

I told her, "Okay", and I hung up the phone.

I called my brother into the house and told him to clean up his room. He went into his room for what seemed like forever. All the while, I didn't bother to check and see if he was cleaning his room. Time had passed, and before I knew it, my mother was pulling up in the driveway. I had forgotten to check my brother's room. I thought that my mother would understand that he was old enough to clean his own room. She came into the house and didn't really speak. In fact, she never spoke. She would never tell me that she loved me. She would tell my brother that she loved him, all of the time. My mother went straight into my brother's room to check it. Enraged, she ran out of the room and slapped me across my face as hard as she possibly could. I could actually see stars. She then went into her room and got a belt, and she commenced to beating me silly. It hurt me so badly. She sent me to my room. I didn't care about eating dinner, because there was never any food in the house. My dad and my mother had gotten separated when I was eleven years old. It didn't really faze me, because he lived around the corner, and he would visit whenever it crossed his mind. I wasn't that close to my father, anyway. The void of him not being there was just fine with me. The next day, my mother had called me, from her salon.

She asked me, "Did you clean your brother's room?"

I didn't know that I was supposed to be a mind reader. I told her that I didn't clean the room. She told me that she was going to beat me when she got home. Lord knows that I didn't want another beating like the one I'd received the day before. After I hung up the phone, I was in a panic. I didn't know what to do, but I couldn't go through this abuse every day. I was getting abused for no reason. I did the only thing that came to my mind, at the time. I grabbed a bottle of aspirin that was on our living room bar and I poured some into my hand. I took the collection of pills, I swallowed them all, and I went to sleep. I guess my mother had gotten home too late to think about the room. The household was asleep, and I had school the next morning. I don't know how I did it, but I woke up the next morning. To my surprise, I was blind! Thank God, it was temporary. I had to sit up in bed and blink for a while. My eyes started working again. I had the biggest headache in the world. My head was spinning, and I had to get up and get dressed for school. I had forgotten that it was picture day, and I grabbed the first wrinkled thing that I could find. I was going to put it on before I had to take the picture. I went to school and I didn't feel very well.

My teacher asked, "Are you okay?"

I began to cry. She sent me to the school counselor, and I told her about my taking the pills. She enrolled me in the school's weekly drug abuse program and notified my mother. My mother must have been too busy to come right away, because she let the day go by. She came home, when she knew that I was out of school. She tried to talk to me.

She asked me, "Why did you try to kill yourself?"

I told her, "I did it because you don't love me. I'm not needed here, because you have my brother."

She told me that she loved me and whatever else she could think of to cover up her not being there for me. Time passed and she began dating different men. I was sick of it. It's bad enough that she didn't pay me any mind. She was neglecting me and my brother for these bastards. One particular beau that she had, crawled under my skin. He was in his early *twenties* and in the military. There was something about him that I just didn't like. He looked just like a rat in the face. Sooner than later, his rat-faced tactics came into play. He had brought up a thought, to my mother that was very disturbing to me. He had told her that he thought that I may have wanted him in a sexual manner. She accused me of wanting to have sex with him. No mother should be on this subject with her daughter. No mother should bring different men in and out of the house, around her kids. I blew her off, and I went into my place of peace—my room. The next morning, my mother called me from her salon and asked to speak to my brother. I gave him the phone and walked off. Apparently, she asked him if I had cleaned his room. Naturally, his response was *no*.

He gave the phone back to me and stuck his tongue out at me saying, "You're in trouble. Ha, ha!"

I had gotten back on the phone, and my mother didn't give me a chance to speak. All I heard was her yelling and her saying that she was going to beat me for not cleaning up my brother's room. She hung up. I was so mad and tired of her evil ass. I went into the kitchen, I grabbed a bottle of pills, and I gulped them down with a glass of water. I just wanted my life to be over. I wanted her to see how life would be without me to treat badly, anymore. In the midst of taking the pills and crying furiously, I didn't realize that my brother was watching me. I blew him off, went into his room, and I began to clean the pig sty up. Later that evening, my mother came home. I was in my room, as usual. Her raggedy ass boyfriend was there, so was my little brother. I guess she had given my brother his hug and kiss, as she always did, and asked him what he did for the day. He went straight to telling her that he saw me taking some pills. She burst into my room and began yelling at me. She kept asking me why I kept trying to end my life. I didn't get a chance to respond. She started punching me as hard as she possibly could. All I could do was cry. I was so drugged up, on pills, that I couldn't feel any of her punches. In all of the rage and chaos, I caught a glimpse of her boyfriend standing in my doorway. The clown was laughing and watching her punch and beat me. Damn! I could've killed the both of them. Thank God that I didn't.

My mother didn't realize that her control over me was making me miserable. Before I could leave with Zic, my mother gave him a long lecture on stressing me out. She told him that I didn't need to be stressed, for the baby's sake. He gave her his head nods and agreement tones, and we went on our way. We had finally gotten home, and I was exhausted. All I wanted to do was crawl into the bed and go to sleep. Unfortunately, that wasn't on Zic's agenda. He had a different motive. You guessed it! He wanted to have sex. I could barely stand being under the same roof of his abusive ass, let alone him touching me, in any manner. I had no love for that low life asshole. Damn. Why couldn't he just keel over and die? I sat my son on our bed, and began to get ready for bed. I put some clothes on, and I climbed into bed. Zic sat at the edge of the bed, and he gestured me to sit up and talk to him.

I told him, "I'm tired. I don't feel like talking."

He replied, "Well, let's fuck."

I said, "No."

He then yanked my arm and pulled me towards him. I was crying so much, that I could feel my eyes puffing up. He kept telling me to shut up, but I just kept crying. All kinds of thoughts were running through my head. All of that went on, while the baby was sitting and watching. He was at his crawling age, so he couldn't understand what was being said. Zic told me to shut up, and he slapped me across my face. I slapped him back. He slapped me harder. I slapped him harder. He slapped me, threw me on the bed, snatched my clothes off, and penetrated me, with force. My son was still on the bed watching his pregnant mother get raped, by his dad. It hurt so badly. I just cried and cried, until it was over. I never told a soul about what happened that night, until now. The next morning, Zic got up to get ready for work. He got dressed, and he had the nerve to come over to the bed and kiss me goodbye. I turned my head away from his kiss. I had sorrow, in my heart. I wanted to die.

Saturday rolled around, and I caught the bus to work. Hiding my pain had become second nature to me. No one knew the problems that I had to face behind closed doors. That day, something just wasn't sitting right with me. Deep down, inside, I could feel a bad vibe. The phone rang, and my boss answered. She looked at me and told me that the phone was for me. I was thinking that a customer was calling for me. To my surprise, it was my mother. We said hello to one another, and she began to talk. Her voice didn't sound normal. She told me that she had some news to tell me. There was a long pause.

I asked, "What is it?"

She responded by saying, "Momma died, this morning."

My heart dropped, instantly. I couldn't believe it. My Granny passed away. I was supposed to take her driving that summer. She was supposed to hold her second great-grandchild, and she wasn't supposed to leave me. My mother reassured me that it was okay to cry and let it out. I was so distraught. I began to cry and drown in my tears. My boss came over and took the phone away from me. She gave me a hug, and she gave me the rest of the day off. I rode the bus home in sorrow.

When I got home Zic asked, "Why are you home, so early?"

I told him, "My Granny died, this morning."

I began to cry a river. He held me as I let it all out. I broke away from his hold and went into the bedroom to lie down. For hours, all I did was sob in my pillow. My eyes were swollen, and my heart was heavier than my impregnated body. I couldn't move. Zic came into the room for what I thought was to comfort me.

He placed his arm around me and whispered, "Let's have sex. It'll make you feel better."

I said, "No."

I turned over, on my side, making sure not to face him. I could tell that Zic was furious. All I could hear was him huffing and puffing, loudly. He made sure that his anger was known. I felt Zic get up, from the bed, and he walked out of the room. He only left the room for about five seconds. I heard the bathroom cabinet open and close, and Zic reentered the room. He laid on the bed. A few seconds had passed. I tried my best to ignore him jacking off next to me. What a stupid, inconsiderate, and heartless asshole. The nerve of him jacking off while I was grieving and sobbing. If you think that was something to know, wait until you hear what happens next. Upon his finishing jacking off and ejaculating, Zic thought that it would be humorous to reach across me and wipe it all in my face, while he was laughing. I was hurt and humiliated. All I could do was scream, cry and lie there sulking. I wiped my face with a towel that I had found next to the bed.

Zic's laughter stopped, with him saying, "You should've fucked me."

He got up, and he left the room. *What did I get myself into?*

CHAPTER SIX- THE SECOND ADDITION

After attending my Granny's funeral, flashbacks began to cross my mind. I would remember times that my Granny would tell me things like, *"Don't ever let a man put his hands on you."* I would promise her that I wouldn't.

Look at me, now. My Granny's gone, and I was breaking all that I had promised her. I could no longer allow bad things to happen to me. I had quit my job, as time went on, and a few months had passed. I attended and finished the parenting classes. I was also attending the sixteen week domestic violence classes that were ordered. It was a long and hot summer. I was big, pregnant, and miserable. I never missed a DV class. The classes seemed to drag out. There would be a class cancellation or a day reschedule. That threw me off, because I had no phone and couldn't contact the class to check on any of that information. I had to catch the bus. The bus ride would take a total of an hour an half, one-way. On top of that, I couldn't bring my child, because there were no children allowed. My mother had to come and pick my son up, so that he could stay with her. On the bright side, the class delays were perfect for my Ob/Gyn appointments. I didn't have to worry about missing a day or doubling up on catching the bus. Early one morning, during a two week delay, I was awakened by a short and sharp pain, in my abdomen. I didn't think anything of it, and I laid back down. Ten minutes hadn't even passed, when I felt the pain again.

"Oh my God, I think I'm having contractions", I yelled to get Zic's attention.

He was half asleep. I shook him and told him that I was contracting, and the baby may be coming.

Nothing new. Out of his mouth came, "Let's fuck. It'll make it easier for the baby to come."

"What the hell ever", I said.

I got up, and I started pacing around the apartment. The contractions had become seven minutes apart. I waited, and I waited. I timed them, again. I had to wait, because it was too early to knock on a neighbor's door and ask if I could use their phone. By the time a later time had come, I was five minutes apart. I went to a neighbor's house to call an ambulance. I had asked Zic to help me get ready. He lifted his head from the pillow, blew me off, and went back to sleep. It looked like I was going to be in this by myself, as usual. I waited for the ambulance to come and pick me up. The EMT crew came to the door, with a stretcher, but I told them that I was able to walk. I told them that my contractions were five to six minutes apart, and they had been, for a while. The EMT crew timed my contractions and came up with the same number that I had. After my admittance to the hospital, I called my mother and told her that I was going to have the baby. She told me she couldn't make it. After a couple of hours of being in the hospital, Zic showed up. He told me that he had to leave so he could go and find a job. He stayed long enough to see the baby's birth and he left.

Unfortunately, Zic's nosy ass mother worked in the hospital that I was in. She came into the room and asked if she could see the baby. I was holding him, and I wasn't about to let her hold my baby.

She looked at him and said, "Oh! He's cute, Twinky."

As if I made ugly babies. In all actuality, I knew that she was amazed at how light-skinned my son was. He looked just like my Granny. My Granny was light-skinned, and had green eyes. She was so beautiful. I was happy when Zic's mother left my room. My skin crawled, with disgust, whenever she was around. The next couple of hours, I enjoyed the company of my newborn baby. It was just the two of us.

CHAPTER SEVEN- LORD GIVE ME STRENGTH

After about a day, the hospital released me and my baby. I still didn't have a car, so I had to bite my pride and ask Zic's mother for a ride home. The first couple of days, of having the baby home, weren't that bad. He slept quite a bit, which was good for me. My mother still had my oldest son. That was a load off of my plate. One night, Zic decided that we should celebrate my not being pregnant anymore. I put the baby to sleep, while he went out and bought the cheapest wine that he could get. The taste of the wine was good to me. I mixed it with orange juice. That made it taste even better. I drank that whole bottle by myself. I didn't realize how drunk I was, until I got up. I was stumbling and giggling, for a good fifteen minutes. I wanted to go outside and get some air. I stepped down on what I thought was a step. I raised my foot up too high, and I slammed my foot down so hard that I sprained my ankle. I fell on the floor. Zic picked me up and carried me to the bedroom. I thought that I had broken my ankle. I went to sleep, in order to keep the pain off of my mind. The next morning, Zic had to get up and get ready for work. I thought that my ankle would have gotten better overnight. I was wrong. I pulled the covers back, only to find a big and swollen ankle. I tried to stand on it, but it just wasn't working out. Zic had already left for work. The baby started to cry, and I couldn't walk into the room to get him. I had to hop into his room and keep the weight on the uninjured side. I wanted to go into the living room to watch television, but I didn't want the baby in his room. I wanted him to be in my view. I took the baby in my arms. I couldn't hop with him in my arms, so I got down on my hands and knees. While holding the baby in one arm, I proceeded to crawl into the living room. I laid the baby on a blanket that was on the floor of the living room. After a couple of hours of doing this, I couldn't take it anymore. I hopped down the steps, and I went to use a neighbor's phone to call someone to take me to the emergency room.

A few weeks had gone by before my ankle had gotten fully

healed. I started to become more conscious of how my body looked. I started exercising. I would work out, when Zic was at work. His abuse hadn't happened for about a month. That was a miracle in itself. I wasn't going to sit around and guess when it was going to start back up. Zic was so concerned with work and hanging out with his friends, that he hadn't noticed that my body was getting leaner and more toned. I found myself doing Tae Bo twice a day, and I was watching what I ate. My goal was to not let him abuse me anymore. I was going to get stronger and wiser.

One day, on Zic's day off, we had gotten into an argument. I was holding the baby. He was no more than one month old. I tried to calm the yelling, between us, down. All of a sudden, Zic slapped me across my face so hard that my ears were ringing. My face was stinging so badly. I wanted to cry, but I just couldn't let that bastard have the victory over me. I thought to myself, *I was going to get this asshole back, for what he had done to me, over time.*

I closed my eyes, and I said a little prayer. "Lord, give me strength!"

I waited for an hour to pass. I put the baby to sleep and placed him in his crib. My oldest son was already asleep in the room. Zic was sitting on the couch eating and watching television.

I took a deep breath, and I walked over to Zic and said, "That was the last time you will put your hands on me."

Zic replied, "Shut-up, bitch."

He pushed me away from him.

I said, "I didn't put my hands on you, so don't put your hands on me."

I smacked the plate of food that he was eating onto the floor. Zic jumped up and tried to grab at me. I ran into the bedroom. Zic, of course, followed me. I ran around the foot of my king-sized bed to the other side of the room. He chased me like the dummy that he was. I jumped onto the bed as he grabbed at me. I hopped off of the bed, onto the other side, and I ran back down the hallway and into the living room. I only had a split second to think fast. I saw

Zic running towards me. I quickly dropped to the floor, on my back. Zic jumped in mid-air to try to land on top of me, but I was too quick. While he was in the air, I grabbed him by his arms and placed my foot into his chest. All in one motion, I threw him over my head. He slammed into something. I could hear him screech like the girl that he truly was. I didn't have time to worry about him being hurt. I had to, once and for all, teach his ass a lesson. I got up and quickly jumped onto his chest. I immediately grabbed the collar of his shirt, and I began twisting it onto his Adam's apple. I was too quick for him. I was choking him so hard that I could feel a little bit of his life pondering away in my angered hands. All that built up frustration was finally being set free. I wanted to see his life end before my eyes. I had always learned that one should never look a man in his eyes before he dies, or it will haunt you for the rest of your life. I wasn't concerned with those words or that theory.

I looked Zic straight into his eyes (foam had begun to form in his mouth and blood shot to the surface of his eyes) leaned in towards him and whispered, "I wanna kill you so bad, my pussy is throbbing."

It was then, that Zic knew his life was at stake. His eyes had bulged out of the sockets even more. He was grabbing for me, but he couldn't touch me. He was just too weak. He was losing his breath by the second, and I loved every waking moment. I was smiling on the inside. Then, it happened. My conscious kicked in. Thoughts started forming into my head. Killing him wouldn't make the situation better. It would only make it worse. My children wouldn't have a mother or a father, because I would've gone to jail. Zic felt my grip let up. On his last string of hope and what little strength he could muster, he grabbed me and flung me over. He was throwing multiple hits at me. In between his hits, I would get a shot or two in. I wasn't going to be anybody's punk. I was going to go down fighting. Zic and I stood up after a few minutes of him fighting me. We both stood, staring at each other and breathing hard. I kept my little fist balled up. I wasn't about to back down to the bastard, anymore.

He said, "I'm gonna give you about five seconds to get some help."

I said, "Oh, really?"

"Yeah", he replied.

I stood and thought to myself for about two seconds. I went into the kitchen, I opened up the silverware drawer, and I pulled out the biggest knife I could find.

I turned to Zic and said, "I have my help, you faggot. One of us is going away in a body bag. One of us is going away in a cop car, and I'm the one who's going to jail."

All his punk ass could do was walk away. I walked downstairs and knocked on the neighbor's door, across from ours. The neighbor opened the door to find an angry wild-haired woman standing at his door.

I told him, "You'd better come and get this faggot, before I kill him."

The neighbor came outside and told me to calm down. He ran back into his house and he got his wife to come down to talk to me. He went to talk to Zic, while his wife talked to me. She later told me to dress my kids and myself, and she took us for a ride. Her husband took Zic for a ride, in his car. We all met at the apartment, after an hour and a half of driving. They talked to the both of us. They told us about problems that they have faced in their marriage, and how they overcame. The one thing that they forgot was that Zic and I weren't married.

The month of August had passed. It seemed as though the fussing and fighting, between us, had come to a halt. That was good. A couple more months had passed. We had decided that the root, of most of our problems, was money. I decided to walk down the street and apply for a job at a local convenience store. The interview went well. A few days later, the manager called to tell me when to start my training. I was excited about having a job. It was a chance for me to have my own money. I had worked there for a couple of months. Things were going great. I was helping out with the bills, and I was also meeting new people. I finally had an outside life. It felt so great. I enjoyed working the graveyard shift, because it meant that I didn't have to sleep next to Zic. By the time I would get off, it was time for him to go to work. It worked out, wonderfully. My manager would tell me that I was doing a great job. I had learned to be proud of myself. I began meeting some interesting people along the way. I had some good co-workers, too. Three particular people that I worked with helped me see my worth. I'll never forget Ike, Sandy, and Teri. As time passed by, I would tell them about the abuse that I was going through. They would, of course, tell me that I didn't need to go through that and I should leave. They didn't understand. It was not that simple. I didn't have anywhere to go and anyone to lean on. I was like a rock in a hard place.

Days and nights were passing by, and I had developed some sort of a social life. I loved it! I had people that I could call friends. Lord knows I didn't have any of those. I loved my job. I was good at what I did. I felt important there. I had finally gotten a sense of belonging. I had gotten used to the crew that I worked with. I looked forward to the mornings of my graveyard shift, because it meant that Zic would be leaving as I was coming in. That meant that I would have time to rest during the day. There were a few times when I would come home and Zic hadn't changed the babies all night. I was so grateful that they didn't get diaper rash. It was only a matter of time before I would be back on my feet, and I could leave that bastard. I just had to hold out for as long as I possibly could.

KELiCHiA

CHAPTER EIGHT-JEALOUSY ON THE MOVE

Zic was jealous that I had a job. It started to get the best of me. He had a problem with me making my own money. Having my own money meant that I didn't need him, and he didn't have anything to throw in my face. I was helping out with the bills, I was exercising, and I was taking better care of my appearance. I don't think Zic liked that, at all.

A few months of my working at the store became too much for him. Zic would want to have sex before I had to go to work. I didn't want him near me. I would tell him things like *I was tired* and any other excuse that I could think of to tell that clown. He'd tell me that he missed my presence at night. I didn't miss his making me sleep naked beside him, because it was comfortable for him. I didn't miss his abusive hands rubbing up and down the sides of my thighs. After a while, Zic started getting tired of my excuses. One night, I was getting ready for work, and Zic wanted to have sex.

I told him, "No."

That answer was not good enough for him. I had gotten fully dressed, and he decided that I was going to give him what he wanted. He grabbed me and slung me on the bed. I told him I didn't want to do anything. He tried, with all of his might, to take my pants off. I wasn't going to let him. I started fighting, kicking, and screaming at him. He tried to put his hand over my mouth, but I bit his hand as hard as I could. He called me a *BITCH* and persisted with trying to pull my pants off. We had gotten into an awkward position during the tussle. He somehow ended up with his face near my legs. I raised my knee as far up as I could, and I slammed it down against his head as hard as I possibly could. He let out a loud screech. I had burst his lip wide open. He attempted to push my eyeball in as far as he could. I grabbed his finger and pulled it all the way back, away from my eye. He gave up. I finished getting dressed, and I went to work. I checked my eye when I arrived at work. My eye was cherry red, and it was throbbing. That dude was taking this abuse thing too far.

I couldn't continue to live like that. I was heading straight to the

bottom.

CHAPTER NINE-SINKING AND THINKING

It was another year, yet the same stuff was happening. Many people tend to think that things are going to get better in an abusive relationship. Looking back, I have realized that things will only get worse.

Tax refund season had arrived, and there were some things that required arguing over. Zic wanted to claim the kids on his tax returns. I wondered why he should be the one to file them. It's not like he took care of them.

When the kids needed diapers, he would buy cigarettes with his last five dollars, instead of diapers. I still reflect on the times that I didn't have money, and Zic wouldn't buy diapers. I would have to cut up my sanitary napkins and place them inside of a pair of my underwear so that I could put them on the babies. I also had to cut up old t-shirts and use them as diapers. When those

78

resources ran out, I would just let them not wear anything at all.

We argued about the filing situation more and more. Tired of arguing and fighting, I gave in. I let him file the kids. When Zic received the money, from the returns, I didn't see him until the next morning. He had cashed the check, and he had gone to hang out with his friends. That low-life piece of shit! I confronted him about giving me part of the money, and he told me that I didn't deserve to get anything because he supports the family. I wanted to kill him. He asked me why I needed money. I wanted to purchase a car for myself. He also wanted to purchase a car. He told me that we couldn't afford to take care of two cars. The next day, he arrived with a car that he had purchased from someone. I forgot how much his truck cost, but it wasn't worth it. I didn't pay him any mind, for a few days. I was still working and doing what I had to do to survive for me and my kids. One afternoon, Zic told me to start pricing a car for myself. I was very happy to hear that. After a couple of weeks of searching, I had found a car that suited my budget. I didn't have to walk through the woods to get to work, anymore. I had a car of my own. It was a well-deserved accomplishment. I was doing well with working and maintaining the car payments. It all came to a halt, when I could no longer afford to have insurance on the car. Like most folks would do, I continued to drive the car without insurance. That didn't matter to me, anyway. Nothing good was meant to come my way. It seemed like someone had it out for me. I wasn't going to amount to anything in life.

Every day became another day for thoughts of leaving that situation behind me. I wanted to get out of that lifestyle so badly, it hurt. On one of my days off, Zic and I had an argument about something. I can't remember the exact facts that triggered the argument. I can remember leaving him and my sons in the house. I drove to the store that I worked at to talk to someone and to get away from Zic. I started talking to Teri, who was working at the time. Next thing I knew, everyone's attention was focused outside. I had only caught a glimpse of what looked like Zic's truck speeding out of the parking lot. I ran outside to see why all of the people were standing around looking at my car. I ran to the back of the car.

The bastard had rammed his truck into the back of my car. I knew I

didn't have insurance, so I didn't bother to call the police. I hopped

into my car, backed out of the parking space, and drove off to catch

up with the dummy. I pulled into the complex and didn't give the

car a chance to stop rolling. I threw the gear into park, jumped out

of my car, and I ran into the apartment. He threatened to hurt me

and the kids, if I thought about leaving him. I told him that he

wasn't going to do anything to us. We argued, back and forth. I put

the kids in their room, so they wouldn't have to witness us arguing

and fighting. I knew that was where we were headed. I had to brace

myself. I was ready for that moment. I had been building myself up

for that moment. Another hour had passed, and the room was

getting heated with evil emotions. We began throwing things at

each other. He threw an ashtray that hit me in my pelvic area. I

screamed loudly, hoping that someone would hear.

Zic must have gotten scared, and told me to, "Shut up."

I told him, "I don't have to do anything that I don't want to do."

Wham! He had punched me on the right side of my face, as hard as he possibly could. I felt the muscles, in my face, swell instantly. I could hear the ligaments stretching, beyond control. I was shocked that he even took it that far, and he was shocked that he didn't knock me out, on his first punch. Zic used to be a boxer, and he used to knock guys out on the first hit.

I grabbed my face and I started screaming to the top of my lungs, "Help! Fire!"

I learned never to scream what you really need help for, because people wouldn't respond as fast. He yelled for me to shut-up, but I didn't. The bastard needed to pay for the pain he had ever put me through. Reality had set in, for him. If the police were to see the damage that he had done to my face, he'd definitely be grabbing his behind to keep it from getting taken. He began crying, frantically. He grabbed me and started apologizing and hugging me. We both became very quiet.

He then said, "We have to get out of the house for a while."

We both knew that the police would have a field day with him and the kids. We got dressed, dressed the kids, and headed for the door. When the front door was opened, there stood the county's finest. They began asking questions about the arguing and stating that they were called by neighbors. Zic tried to walk away from them, but two of the officers followed him and tried to get answers out of him. The officer that stayed with me knew me from the store that I worked at. He asked me if everything was alright. Of course, I lied to him. I told him that everything was just fine. He me asked if he could inspect my body for markings. I told him that I didn't have a problem with that. I had put on a baseball cap and pulled it as low as possible, so that my face wasn't visible. It was dark outside. The officer had to shine a flashlight in my face. The bruise was on the right side of my face. I had turned so that the officer could only see the left side of my face and body. He missed the right side of my body, said *okay*, and walked off. I was relieved. The other two officers were still questioning Zic. He wasn't liked very much. He had walked back towards me and our youngest child. Zic was holding the oldest child in his arms. He had a look of disgust on his face. I didn't know why he looked disgusted. I was the one with the swollen face. We got into my car and took a drive to a secluded area to talk.

I had to work the next day. I wore my baseball cap and kept the right side of my face turned away from people. I tried so hard to hide my bruises and hurt from others. My esteem was so low. The end of my shift came around, and my manager arrived to do her daily preparations. She came out front to gather the money from the safe. I guess she had seen a glimpse of my face and called me into her office. She asked me about my face and what was going on at home. I broke down and told her about the abuse that I was going through, every day. I told her that was the reason why I had been calling out all of the time. She told me that I needed to make a decision about my life—not only for myself, but for my children. I told her that I would do just that. I went home. Zic was up and getting ready for work. He apologized for hitting me, and he kissed me on my right cheek. I blew him off and was happy to see him leave. I changed the children's diapers, gave them a bath, and fed them. I knew that I couldn't count on Zic to do that. I put the babies down to sleep, and I began brainstorming. A few hours of thinking had gone by, and I decided to get the kids dressed and packed as many of my things as my little car could hold. I didn't tell any of my neighbors what was going on. I packed all of the towels, washcloths, toilet paper, and much more. I strapped the babies in their car seats, jumped in the car, and I drove off. I stopped by my job and talked to the manager. She told me to do what I had to do. I asked her if I could keep my job. She told me that I could. She also said that she would try to get me a transfer close to where I was going. I got into the car, and I drove to my hometown.

CHAPTER TEN-ON THE GRIND

I arrived at my mother's house, and I asked her if the kids and I could stay with her. She let us stay, but only for a little while. After about a week or two, she told me that I had to go, because she couldn't risk getting put out of her apartment. We couldn't stay, because we weren't on her lease. How low can a person get? That's pretty low. I got my kids, put them into their car seats, and got into the car.

My mother followed me, and she asked, "Where are you going?"

I told her, "Don't worry about us. We aren't on your lease."

I left and drove around for hours. I didn't have anywhere to go. I didn't have much money. I was living off of my last paycheck. I had a few diapers for the kids. Nighttime grew, and I

86

KELiCHiA

was tired. I couldn't think of anywhere to go. I drove to a parking

lot that was fairly empty. I parked the car, made sure that the kids

were comfortable, laid my seat back, and I went to sleep. I woke

up, after about two hours. I couldn't sleep over the sounds of the

eighteen wheelers that were gathered in the parking lot. I

checked on the babies to make sure that they were okay. They

were still asleep. As long as they were comfortable, I was okay.

The morning had rolled around, and I had to get us bathed. I

stopped by a store on the way to my next quest. I had to find

somewhere to stay. I bought a couple of twenty five cents snacks

and a gallon of water. My driving journey ended at a local beach

parking lot. At least I could enjoy the scenery, while I

contemplated on what I was going to do to keep us safe. I found a

container of baby wipes and emptied it. I poured water, from the

water jug, in it and used it as a basin. I used that water to bathe

the babies. This water had to last me for as long as possible. I

needed the money I had for gas. I sat in the car, at the beach, for

what seemed like forever.

Nightfall came around, again. I found myself back at the store's parking lot. I did this routine for two weeks. Something had to give. I couldn't do this any longer. I found my way to my great-aunt's home. I talked to her for a while. I didn't tell her what I was going through. I didn't want to burden anyone else. Besides, I wasn't on anyone's lease, and I didn't want to get anyone into trouble. My great-aunt ended up telling me that my aunt lived a few doors down, from her, and my cousins were visiting her. I decided to walk to my aunt's apartment. She wasn't there, but my cousins were. I hung out with them for a while. We talked and reminisced about our childhood. We were mothers now, and the childhood memories were long gone. My aunt came home, later that evening, and I explained to her what was going on, in my life. She told me that she couldn't bear to see me and my kids on the street. She invited me to stay with her. It was only going to be temporary. I was going to get a job and pay my aunt half of the rent. My cousins and their children were in the apartment, too. I had found a job at a haircutting salon. The money was okay. The tips were buying my babies' diapers. One of my cousins watched

my kids for me, while I was working. I thought that things were

going great, until my car's engine started making noises. I didn't

know what I was going to do if the car broke down. I wasn't in the

position to afford any mechanical work that had to be done to the

car. I drove around, with the knocking engine, for about two

weeks. I couldn't take staying in an apartment full of people, so I

did what I thought was logical. I went back to Zic. I arrived at the

apartment and knocked on the door. After taking forever, Zic

finally came down the stairs and opened the door. Instead of

opening the door all of the way, he cracked it. He then stepped

outside, to talk to me. That seemed very strange.

I asked, "Can the kids and I come back to stay? We don't

have anywhere to go, and we have been sleeping in the car."

He told me, "Yes. Go and get the kids out of the car, while I

straighten the apartment."

I thought to myself, *what is he trying to hide, from me?* I went towards the door, and Zic tried his best to block me from coming into the apartment. I somehow got around him, and I darted up the stairs. To my surprise, there was a girl in the apartment. The girl was a sixteen year old, that I saw every now and then, hanging around the teenaged females that were across the way. I immediately jumped towards her, so I could beat her upside her head. Zic grabbed me to protect her from getting her ass kicked. All of my anger turned toward Zic. I started hitting him.

He started yelling, "I thought that you weren't coming back, because it had been so long!"

He reminded me that the kids were still in the car. I had forgotten all about them. I went downstairs to go and get the kids. I was faced with a small group of teenage females. They all seemed to be holding weapons, in their hands, as if they were going to jump me. I didn't give a damn about those little bitches. There was only one female that was on my agenda. The bitch's name was Darlene. I spotted her, when I looked to my left. I darted so fast, that no one was able to catch me to hold me back. When I reached Darlene, something came over me. Instead of punching the bitch in her face, I told her that what she did was wrong. I fed all kinds of bullshit to her. I told her that I was deeply hurt and I thought that she was my friend. I was telling her all sorts of emotional lies. Her guilty conscious made her cry. She started telling me that she was sorry and she didn't want to lose what friendship we had. I really don't know what she was thinking, but I pick and choose who I call friends, very carefully. She was definitely was no friend of mine. I told her that if I caught her again, she was going to have hell to pay.

I thought that things were going to be a little bit different being back in the household with Zic. For a while we didn't speak. Time passed at a slow pace, and I only worked a few days a week at the salon. My car was giving me more and more problems. Something had to give. One day, on the way to work, my car had broken down. I was half way in between the apartment and the salon. I was about fifteen minutes away from either of them.

Someone had pulled over to help me. They allowed me to use their cell phone. The first thing I did was call my job to tell them that I couldn't make it in. I told the manager that I was having problems with my car. She told me that was no excuse for not being able to get to work. She told me that I was already late, and I was calling late. She told me that I had better get to work within the next couple of hours, or don't bother to come back. Well, what the hell was I supposed to do? I had no other choice. I had no money and no way to get to work. I just didn't show up. I didn't like that dumb ass manager anyway. I was only putting up with her for the sake of my kids. I managed to get a ride home, from someone. When I arrived home, Zic was laying on the couch.

He asked, "Why are you home so early?"

I told him what happened and left it at that. A few weeks had gone by, and I grew tired of being there, again. I just didn't feel right. I didn't even like to lay in my bed, because Zic had sex with that young girl in it. Not to mention, I found out that Zic also had sex with another sixteen year old, in my bed. I couldn't seem

to shake those thoughts off. I decided to leave him, again. I went

back to my aunt's home, where my cousins and their children

were staying. I had given up hope on any type of descent life for

myself and for my sons. I had made up, in my mind, I wasn't going

to amount to anything. I had come to the conclusion that my life

was going to be unsuccessful. My younger cousin, of the two, and

I began to hang out together. I would drive my engine knocking

car to wherever it would take us. I began to get a little taste of the

streets. I got to see what was really going on in the world. I had

been living a sheltered life up until that point. One day, my engine

finally went dead, and I called the dealership that I had bought

the car from. I told the salesman that the engine was shot, and I

told him where I had left the car. The good thing about that

situation was that the owner of the dealership had decided not to

place the repossession on my credit.

   A couple of months had passed, and my cousin and I were

having the time of our lives. We didn't have jobs, but we still managed to have fun and make the best out of a bad situation.

We'd begun meeting people on a daily basis. My cousin had met a

couple of guys, at a local store. She'd invited them to come and

drink at the apartment. One of the guys, that she'd met, stayed in

the same complex. He told us that he had a female roommate,

and he was tired of living with her. We all laughed at the things

that he would tell us. As the night continued on, we began to like

the presence of these guys, more and more. They were really cool

and down to earth. The partying and hanging out went on for

days and weeks. One day, we were all sitting at the kitchen table,

and there was a knock at the door. In walks a young, light skinned

guy. He called for Darren to come out and talk to him. Darren was

one of the guys that my cousin and I were hanging out with.

Darren came back inside, after a couple of minutes of being gone.

Darren didn't even get a chance to sit down at the table good,

when my cousin and I started asking questions about his guy

friend. He gave us a little smile. He told us that was his roommate.

I responded, "I thought you said that you had a female roommate."

He said, "I know that I told y'all that I had a female roommate. That's her!"

We couldn't believe it. Our eyes were bulging, and our mouths had dropped to the floor. She looked exactly like a boy. She had on a wife beater, khaki shorts, and she had a fade that was tighter than Martin Lawrence's. She had a flat chest. That's why we couldn't tell what her sex was. She pulled the boy look off really well. It was almost to perfection. A few days of hanging out had passed, and Darren's roommate began to hang out with us. We had finally gotten used to her. She was sort of cool to hang around. My cousin still kept her distance, because she was very homophobic. Days and nights had passed, and we were getting bored with the routine of sitting at home. Darren's roommate was named Sheena. Sheena had asked us if we'd ever attended a private party. We told her *no*. She invited us to attend one that she was having. She pulled me to the side and asked me if I would like to entertain at the party. At first, I thought that she meant singing. She told me later on that she wanted me to dance. I told her that I would think about it, and I would get back with her. I told my cousin what Sheena had proposed to me. My cousin told me that I should go for it. She told me that I had the body for it and if she had the body, she'd definitely do it. I explained to my cousin, Tisha, that I didn't know how to dance or be sexy. She showed me what moves to make and how to be sexy and exotic with my moves. I sure was glad that I had her to teach me. That point in my life was my exploration stage. I hadn't really experienced anything. I had been tied down with kids and living the family life. I never had the chance to be a party animal.

The private party was starting, and Sheena was nowhere to be found. I was not going to perform by myself. She had to be out of her mind. Tisha had deemed herself as my bodyguard. I was happy to have her there with me. Finally, Sheena showed up to the party. She was late to her own house party. The private party was held at her house. She pointed me in the direction of her room. We all went back there. Her room was the changing area. She explained about being nervous and not to worry. Nothing was going to happen that I didn't want to happen. She went to the front room to tell the DJ when to play her music. Tisha had only showed me how to dance, slowly. I requested all slow songs. Sheena's music began to play, and all of my butterflies started fluttering. Tisha tried to talk me out of my nervousness, but it didn't work. All of a sudden, Sheena's music had stopped playing, and a slow song began to play. She came back into the changing area. She didn't have on any clothes. My nervousness went out of the window. I told her that I was not about to take my clothes off for anyone. She told me that I didn't have to. I could go out there and do whatever I felt. I stayed in costume. I went into the front room, where all of the men were. The feeling of all eyes on me was overwhelming. I was in control of the whole situation. I felt like a queen. One of the men became kind of obsessed with me. He immediately grabbed me, so that I could dance for him, personally. I sat on his lap and began to grind my hips back and forth. He started throwing money at me. I was letting the situation control me. I suddenly got some sort of a conscience, and I got up. I left the front room and went into the changing area. I opened my hand up and threw the money that I had grabbed onto the bed. I thought that I would like doing something like that, but I was wrong. I felt lower than the lowest being. I felt degraded. That wasn't something that a mother should do. On the other hand, I was doing what I had to do to feed my kids. I started getting on the grind. I tried the dancing thing a few more times that night, but the money wasn't cutting it. The men were cheap as hell. I had to stop. I finally told Sheena that I was quitting. She understood. She had pulled me to the side and confessed that she wanted me in a sexual manner. I told her that I didn't sleep with women.

She said, "All I need is a few minutes alone with you. I promise, once you try me, you won't go back to men."

I blew her comment off.

"Whatever", I said.

She later asked me if she could kiss me. She told me that she had always wanted to kiss me.

I asked, "What could be the harm? I guess it would be okay."

No harm in a kiss. Besides, I wanted to satisfy my small inkling of curiosity. She kissed me, and I kissed her back. It didn't feel too bad. In fact, I kind of enjoyed it. Needless to say, I later found myself in her bedroom, without clothes any clothes on.

CHAPTER ELEVEN- SAME BOAT, DIFFERENT RIVER

Well, I guess that I couldn't cut it in the real world. I found myself crawling back to that low down, dirty shame called Zic. I had no other place to go. I had no other choice. It's almost like I didn't have a mind of my own. He had control over the little brain that I did have left. Things were going good for a little while, but I was back in the same boat of having no money and nothing to call my own. Something had to give. One day, I took the kids for a stroll. We walked to the shopping center that was about two miles up the road. I had gone to just about every store and filled out an application. I had gone to a store that I used to work in, but they were under new management. It wasn't guaranteed that I was going to get that job back. About three months had passed, and I was fed up with this lifestyle. On Zic's day off, I began to do a lot of thinking. I had thought about my life and my children's lives. I just couldn't go on living with this bum. He was worthless.

KELiCHiA

He wasn't worth the dirt at the tip of my fingernails. I had to think

of something. I just couldn't stay any longer. I brainstormed a

good lie, in my head, to tell him. I threw on some clothes, got the

children dressed, and I grabbed a baby bag. I stuffed it with

whatever I could find. He had mentioned that since it was his day

off, he wanted to hang out with his friends. That was perfect. I

told him that I was going to take the kids over his brother's

girlfriend's house, while I went to go and check on a few job

applications. I left. I took the bus to her house. I refused to look

back. I only had the clothes that were on my back and what I had

packed in the baby bag for the kids. I arrived at Shelly's house. She

let me in and asked what was wrong with me. I told her that that

was the last straw.

"I just can't stand to look at his face another minute", I

told her.

I couldn't live with that abuser any longer.

She told me, "I understand. What are you going to do?"

I responded, "I'm gonna have to swallow my pride and ask my mother if I could stay with her for a little while."

Not realizing it, a few hours had passed by, and Shelly and I were still talking. She told me to do what I had to do to take care of my children. Suddenly, there was a knock at the door. Shelly opened the door, and her face drew blank. She looked over at me and told me that Zic wanted to talk to me. I told her that I didn't have anything to say to him.

She looked at him, and he said, "I just want to talk to her."

I got up and stood at the doorway. Zic told me to come with him, to go home. I told him that I didn't want to and it was over. I told him that I was sick and tired of the lifestyle that we were living. Zic was wearing a brown pullover, with no shirt underneath, and a raggedy pair of blue jeans. He was holding a cigarette in his hand. He began to get frustrated at my rejections.

He said, "I'm gonna say it one more time. Let's go!"

Again, I said, "No!"

He then placed the cigarette in his mouth, took a deep breath, and yanked me out of the doorway. I tried my best to get out of his grip. Shelly was screaming for him to let me go.

"Let her go, Zic! She said she doesn't want to go with you!"

Zic wasn't trying to hear anything that Shelly had to say. Suddenly, a door in the house had flung open, and Zic's brother ran out. He was in the bedroom sleeping the whole time. Zic had managed to rip my shirt off of me. He tried his best to throw me down the stairs of the apartment building. Zic's brother, Mike, went straight for his collar. His brother was a little bit bigger than Zic's six foot, 210 pound frame. He had Zic up and off of the ground. His feet were afloat, with the rest of his body.

He began yelling at Zic.

"Man, she said she didn't want to go with you!"

Zic told Mike that he didn't want to fight him. I was

thinking, *he doesn't want to fight his match, but his punk ass will fight a woman.*

The police arrived, at the residence within five minutes of the altercations. Zic made his way downstairs, and somehow, his nosy ass mother had made it to the complex. Zic told his two cents to the officers, and he thought that I was going to do the same. I was at the end of the rope with his stupid ass. He needed to pay for all of the hurt he bestowed upon me and my sons. The police came upstairs to get information from me. I peeked downstairs and caught a glimpse of Zic pacing back and forth. His mother was right alongside him. The officer began to ask me questions about the situation. I didn't tell him that he tried to throw me down the stairs, but I did want Zic scared out of his mind. I informed the officer that Zic grabbed my arms, and I snatched away. It was an unwanted touch. This seemed like déjà vu. The police officer confirmed my story. All that he needed to hear was who touched who. He explained that the call came in as two men fighting. I explained to him that Mike was taking up for me. He was

protecting me from Zic. The officer went down the stairs, and Zic

was still pacing back and forth. I know he was thinking that I was

going to lie for him, like I always did. He had another thing

coming. Trying to be cool, Zic walked over to the officer. I was

watching everything from the top of the stairs. The officer began

to read Zic his rights, and Zic started having a fit. He was resisting

arrest. Two more officers came over, to help the other one. They

just couldn't keep Zic under control. He struggled and struggled.

One more officer came over. They were finally able to contain and

restrain Zic. They cuffed him and threw him into the back seat of a

squad car. Zic was kicking and yelling. He tried his best to kick the

window out of the car. His mother kept asking the officers what

he'd done wrong. He was being charged with assault and battery.

Zic spent a day, or so, in jail. His mother picked him up

from the jailhouse and brought him back to Shelly's house. The

kids and I had stayed there for the duration that Zic was confined.

Zic also had to pick up his truck that was there. He had no

business driving it. A couple of months prior to that particular incident, Zic was charged with a hit and run and driving without insurance. His license was suspended, and he wasn't supposed to be driving. The assault and battery charges were the icing on his cake. Zic was still in complete shock. We drove home in silence. He had gotten dressed, and he went to work. When Zic arrived home, later that evening, he was still in shock.

He said, "I can't believe that they put me in a cell with a murderer."

I didn't believe the shit that was coming out of his punk ass mouth.

I replied, "A crime is a crime. No criminal is better or worse than the next one."

I left it at that.

Time began to fly. October had flown by, quickly. November through February had flown by, also. The month of March 2001 was finally here. Zic's court appearance, for the assault and battery charge, was in that month. Over the few months that flew by, Zic and I didn't really associate. He would go his way, and I would go mine. Zic got up, got dressed, and went out the door. My mind was going crazy. I wondered what could be the possible outcome. Zic came home a few hours later. He called me into the living room.

"We need to talk", he said.

"About?" I saw it coming.

"Maybe it's best that we separate. One of us is going to end up getting hurt."

I told him, "I couldn't agree, more!"

Zic was thinking that I was going to be stubborn Twinky and demand to stay. At the same rate, I thought he was going to apologize, like he always did. He didn't. I just starting packing without saying another word. I later called my mother and told her that it was finished. I could no longer live the way that I was living. I had to go!

CHAPTER TWELVE-FROM HUSTLIN' TO FLOWIN'

I found myself living with my cousin, Tisha. She had moved to the downtown area of where I was from. The area was filled with drug dealers and drug users. It was filled with people that had dreams but weren't fulfilling them. Many of the residents had the potential of being successful, but they just weren't applying themselves. They all seemed to be content with living below the means of the community. They had no intentions on bettering themselves. I wasn't exposed to much of that type of lifestyle growing up. I was sheltered for the majority of my adolescence. Seeing all of the things that were going on around me was foreign to me. When I first went to stay with my cousin, I looked terrible. My hair was never combed, properly. I'd let my appearance go. One of the first things that my cousin did was braid my hair. When she was finished, I felt like a brand new person. For the first time, in a long time, I felt like a woman. I didn't realize how beautiful I was, until I looked in the mirror. I almost didn't recognize myself.

After Tisha had finished braiding my hair, we decided to walk to the corner store. On the way there, I stopped at a pay phone to call Zic. I begged him to let me and the kids come back to stay with him. He kept telling me that it wouldn't be a good idea. I begged him for about ten more minutes, and we hung up. Tisha had overheard the conversation that went on.

She said, "Girl, you don't need his no good ass. Fuck him!"

I was hurt for a little while but eventually found myself forgetting about Zic. I had no job, and I had to support my kids. I went to the Social Services office, and I had applied for state assistance. I had to give the Social Worker all of Zic's information, so that the state could file for child support against him. After a month of waiting, I began receiving the temporary assistance checks. The monthly check was about three hundred dollars. I had to use the money, wisely. I was also receiving food stamps. I received about three hundred dollars-worth of food stamps, monthly. My cousin was also receiving assistance from the state. I thought that I could get used to living like that.

One day, my cousin and I were walking to the store, when we saw a cute guy standing on the block.

My cousin said, "Oooo, Twinky. He's cute!"

I then told her that I was going to hook her up with him. She just smirked, and we kept walking towards the store. On the way back, the guy was still standing outside. I yelled over and asked him how old he was.

He asked me, "Who wants to know?"

I told him that I wanted to know, and I was asking for my cousin's sake. He asked my cousin's age.

I told him, "She's 19."

He responded by saying, "I'm 19, too."

I left the conversation at that. I went back and gave Tisha a report on his information. The day had passed and nighttime fell. Tisha and I would always sit on her porch to talk and drink. We'd drink the cheapest alcohol that we could afford. We drank things like MD 20/20 and Andre. We didn't have much, but we'd find ways to have fun.

Tisha and I decided to have a small get together and invite our close circle of friends over. We needed a few more drinks and snacks, so Tisha walked to the store to buy them. On the way, she saw the cute guy that we'd seen earlier in the week. She invited him to our get together. He seemed cool, and she was trying to kick some game to him. The last of all of the invitees arrived at *eleven*. We partied like there was no tomorrow. Time flew, and before we knew it, the party was over. Everyone went home, and Tisha and I cleaned up so that we wouldn't have to do anything the next afternoon.

We woke up the next afternoon and began our routine of sitting on the porch and drinking. Eric came by while we were drinking. Eric is the guy that I was trying to hook up with my cousin. He asked us if he could hang out with us. We told him that it was *cool*. We all sat around and joked all day. Somehow, we got on the subject of Tisha knowing how to braid hair. Eric told us that he needed his hair braided. Tisha told him that he could come by at any time and she'd do his hair. He told her that he would be by later on that night, and he left.

Eric came by like he said he would. Little did he know, Tisha had lost interest in him. She told me that he really wasn't her type. She didn't want to braid his hair, so I ended up doing it. I didn't realize that Eric was only coming by to see me. I learned, later, that he had a crush on me. After a while had passed, Eric and I ended up being a couple. He was a good guy. Even though he was a known drug dealer, he didn't bring that stuff around me and my kids. He would always make sure that we were fed. I later found out that he had lied about his age. He was really *seventeen* turning *eighteen*. It hurt me that he had lied. His mother had a problem at first. She ended up getting used to me, because I kept her son off the streets and out of trouble. His mother and I would go to the club together. She was only in her mid-thirties. She had

Eric at a young age. Things were going good between his family and me. Eventually, I began living with Eric's aunt. She was my age. Tisha and I had a big argument, and I didn't like the way that she was acting towards me and my children. She would blame the filthiness of her house on me and my small kids. It was her daughter who was messing up the house. She also had different men coming in and out of the house. I didn't like that at all. I had gotten a job and had to catch public transportation to get there. I would leave my children at Eric's aunt's house thinking that they would be looked after and cared for, properly. I was wrong. I began finding bruises on either leg of my youngest child. My family was questioning me, as if I was the one putting the bruises on him. I was hurt. I eventually quit that job so that I could be with my kids and monitor them. I'd found that no one could be trusted. I saved one of the state checks that I received, and I purchased a car. It wasn't much, but it was mine. I didn't like that one too much. So, I asked my mother to give me a little more money to put down on another car that I liked. I was able to purchase a luxury car. People began saying that I thought I was better than everyone. I was threatened on a daily basis not to drive down certain roads or I would lose my life. I was stubborn, and I continued to drive wherever the hell I pleased.

I had to get another job. I couldn't just sit around on my ass. One day, I drove to the mall, and I applied for a job at one of the department stores. A few days later, I was called to start training. The job paid once a week. That was perfect. I even got paid for training. Eventually, Tisha and I reconciled. Eric's aunt started getting on my nerves. All she did was smoke weed and drink. I had begun to smoke, too. I did not want to continue to live that lifestyle. I was raised better than that. I asked my cousin if she would baby sit for me while I went to work. She agreed. All the while, I didn't know that a friend of Tisha was abusing my sons. She's lucky that I have outgrown my evil ways, or she wouldn't be breathing right now. After about a month of working at that job, I quit. There had to be a better way of living. I could no longer put my children through that pain and strife.

Morning came, I got up, got dressed, and I left. I went on a journey. At the end of my journey, I found myself at an Air Force recruiting office. The recruiter turned me away, because I was unmarried and had children. I then went to the Marine Corps recruiting office. I was turned away for the same reason. I took a deep breath and went into the Navy recruiting office. The recruiter kindly greeted me and went over the requirements for joining the Navy. He was very kind to me. After he explained everything to me about giving up custody of my children, he asked me what I wanted to do. I told him that I'd think about it, and I'd get back with him. A couple of days had passed and I decided to go back to the Navy recruiting office. The recruiter told me that I had to take a placement test. I told him that it was fine. He had me take a practice test, and I scored high. He was excited, and he told me that I should have no problem passing the actual test. He scheduled an appointment for me to test.

I arrived at the testing center. I was nervous. After several

116

hours, I was finished. Everyone that took the test was instructed to wait for the test results. I waited, and I passed with flying colors. I was very proud of myself. The recruiter contacted me later on that week and told me that I had to schedule a court date to give custody of my children to someone. From there, I contacted my mother and told her that I was planning on joining the military. She told me that nothing else was going on in my life. I explained to her what the recruiter had told me about giving up custody of the kids. She said she'd keep them while I was away. I should've known that there were other motives. I went to the court, and a date was set for the custody hearing. The court date was set for thirty days away. I still don't know why Virginia makes people wait that long for custody cases. My mother later came to me and told me that she'd discussed my joining the Navy to a friend of hers that was a medically retired Army Captain. Her friend had advised me to join the Army, because the promotions were quicker and much easier. I really didn't like that my mother and her friends were trying to dictate my life. I blew my mother off, and told her that it was my decision in whatever choice I made. She grew angry and left. On her way out, I told her that I'd see her during court.

I arrived at the Navy recruiting office to talk to my recruiter about job options and my court date. The time was close to noon, and the office was closed. In a way, that was good, because I was having second thoughts about joining the Navy. I couldn't see myself being on a boat for months at a time. Besides, the recruiter had told me that I wouldn't be able to perform the job that I wanted, because women weren't allowed on the submarines. That was a big turn off for me. I'd decided to go and talk to the recruiter, again. That time around, the office was closed. So were the Air Force and the Marine offices. The only office that happened to be opened, during lunchtime, was the Army recruiting office. I curiously wandered into the Army recruiting office. The recruiters welcomed me with open arms. That's no surprise, knowing what I know, now. I ended up deciding to go into the Army.

My custody court date arrived, and temporary custody was given to my mother. I called my recruiter and told him that the custody paperwork was ready. I couldn't believe it. I was joining the Army. I called my social worker and told her to keep those checks, because I was joining the Army. She tried to get into my business and ask a bunch of questions. I hung up the phone. I had, in my mind, that I was going to keep going forward and never look back. People always say to never forget where you come from. I know where I've come from. That life that I was living, on welfare and not having anything, wasn't me. I wasn't raised that way. I was raised to work for what I wanted and had. I had my education and I wasn't going to be one of those lazy ass people who depended on others. I deserved nothing but the best, and my children deserved the best. By the grace of God, we were going to have the best.

CHAPTER THIRTEEN-UNBELIEVABLE CIRCUMSTANCES

Wow. I made it through basic training. I was somebody, and I was proud of myself. I would send money and gifts to my children whenever I got the chance. My first enlistment contract required me not to have custody of my children for my first term, which was *four* years. My mother decided to get assistance from the state, while I was still in training. I wasn't making much money, but I would send her what I could. I wasn't supporting her. I was supporting my sons. In order to file for state assistance, the parents' social security numbers have to be given up. The government stuck me with a back child support bill. It had gotten dated back to when I filed for support against Zic. I was furious. I didn't have much money as it was. I was even more broke. The garnishments from my check had paid off the back support. The garnishments continued to come out of my check. I don't know what the hell my mother was thinking, but she had some nerve calling me and asking me for more money than what she was receiving from the support. She was out of her damn mind. I purchased a car when I was in school for my military job training. The insurance was really high. Having to pay the support became too much. I had to let my insurance lapse, in order to have a little money to save. I thought that my life was going down the drain, once again. My mother was becoming more and more greedy, and I was sick of it.

I arrived at my first duty station, Fort Drum, New York, in the fall of 2002. I adapted pretty quickly. I thought that being the new soldier on the block was going be a tough hurdle to get over. There were plenty of hounds for me to choose from, but I chose to stay to myself.

A month into my stay, I started talking to a guy that I'd met at one of the clubs on the base. He was a very sweet guy. Unfortunately, he wasn't going be stationed there long. He was getting out of the military. I decided not to get too caught up into that guy. We had gotten physically involved on one occasion. He left a couple of weeks later, and we never kept in touch. I wasn't at the unit long before I had to participate in a field exercise that the unit had to do in Louisiana for a month. When we returned, I began to hang out with a female that had introduced herself to me before we'd gone to Louisiana. A supervisor, which was in my platoon, took interest in me. I was somewhat interested in him. I wasn't sure at that time. I really just wanted to have fun and live life to the fullest. He and I became involved. Having sex with him was miserable. I could never get turned on by him, and that made the sex dry as hell. He made me want to stop having sex, forever. Needless to say, our physical meetings were short-lived.

Our unit had to go back to Louisiana for another month. It was so dreadful down there, because it was hot as hell. About half way through the mini-deployment, I met and fell in lust with a sergeant that was in another company that deployed was with my unit. He was muscular, big, and fine. He had a gold tooth and a sexy smile. He made my heart melt. He told me that he wanted to take me on a date when we got back to New York. I told him that it would be nice. I was happy that he had interest in me.

We'd been back in New York for a week, when I got a knock at my door. To my surprise, it was Ronnie. That was the sergeant that promised to take me out when we got back from Louisiana. He came by to talk to me. One thing led to another, and we began to make out. The making out led to him kissing me all over my body and in other places. After Ronnie finished doing the grown up thing with me, he left. He was a wonderful lover. Ronnie and I continued to date and have sex for a couple of months. Then, it happened. Ronnie told me that he didn't want to be in a relationship, because he didn't want to be tied down. I couldn't believe the bullshit that was coming out of his mouth. He could've told me that before we took it further than making out. Even though Ronnie told me that he didn't want to be in a relationship, we continued to have sexual encounters. That was confusing to me. I was still a young woman, and I had a long way to go. I knew that it was over between us when he kissed another woman in front of me. He thought nothing of it. I guess he thought that he was in *mack* mode. I later called him to come into my barracks room. I was furious. How could he kiss a bitch in my face? He arrived to find the stuffed animal he had given me ripped to shreds and a Valentine's Day card torn in half. I told him that he was a dog and some other words and told him to leave. I told him that I wanted nothing else to do with him.

The year 2003 was another turning point, in my life. I had begun frequenting clubs with the few friends that I had. We would hang out every weekend, without fail. We decided to go to one of the clubs that was on the base, but my car wasn't working properly. I had to ride with a friend. Unfortunately, there wasn't enough room. My friend made me sit on some guy's lap. I didn't know him at all. I did know that he was a new soldier in the unit. I asked him if I was too heavy. He told me that he was just fine. We all had a blast that night. We partied, danced, and drank the night away.

The next day, I'd had enough. I wanted to have a companion.

I went into my homeboy's room. He was asleep. I didn't know that his roommate was the guy whose lap I had sat on the night before. I decided to ask him if he had any male friends that I could talk to. He thought about it and told me that he didn't have anyone to talk to. I knew that was a hint. We asked each other what was up with us linking up. We told each other we'd see each other around, and I left. A week had gone by, and I received a knock at my door. I wondered who the hell could've been knocking at my door. I opened the door, and it was the cutie pie that I was interested in knowing more about. His name was Jeremy. Jeremy asked me if I was busy. I told him that I was getting ready to go out. I invited him in and told him that he could have a seat on the other bed that was in the room. I finished getting dressed, while we talked, and I went out with some friends.

Karma is a true *bitch*. Jeremy and I hung out every day for a few weeks. A group of us decided to go to the club. We all wanted to unwind like we always did. My ex-boyfriend, Ronnie, happened to be there. He even had the nerve to try and talk to me. I ignored him and took Jeremy on the dance floor. We danced to a slow song. I noticed that Ronnie was standing to the side watching Jeremy and me dance. To make the situation better, for me, I gave Jeremy a long and passionate kiss. I could tell that Ronnie was pissed off and jealous. The song ended and Jeremy went to sit down. I was walking toward the table when a hand grabbed my arm and snatched me. It was Ronnie.

He whispered in my ear, "So that's your new man?"

I said, "None of your damn business. Get the fuck outta my face."

I left and went to the table that Jeremy was sitting at. He began to tell me that he really liked me and he thought that I was a very cool person. I took my compliments and left it at that. I still had feelings for Ronnie for some odd reason. Maybe I was used to being treated like shit. I really don't know what it was.

One day, I got a call from my aunt. She told me that she had my children with her. My mother had gone into the hospital. She had become depressed, and she was admitted into a mental hospital. She'd dropped my children and my little brother off at someone's house and walked about *twenty* miles, for no apparent reason. My aunt kept calling my company commander and saying that she couldn't take care of my kids, because they were interfering with her schedule and her life. I was hurt. I didn't know what to do. I ran back upstairs to my barracks room. I was crying. I'd gotten a knock at the door. It was Jeremy. He entered the room and asked me if I was okay. I told him the news that I had heard, and I said that I would be alright. He told me that he would be around if I needed to talk and he left. I thought that was the sweetest thing. Days had gone by, and I would receive notes under my door telling me that I was a cutie and other things. The notes were written by Jeremy.

My commander became restless and told me that she was

going to put me on a weekend pass so that I could go and get my

children from my aunt. She and my supervisors were sick and

tired of my aunt calling my job. They figured that my family wasn't

worth shit, and none of them was really trying to help me. I

thought that if my aunt was so tired of having my kids why she

didn't just bring them to New York. I wasn't in any position to

travel *ten* to *twelve* hours. My car was broken down, and I lived in

the barracks. I was still a Private and wasn't very established. The

next day, my platoon surprised me. They had taken up a collection

to help get my car fixed. They'd collected close to *four hundred*

dollars. I wanted to cry, so badly, but I held the tears back and

thanked everyone. I had my car towed to a shop and paid for the

part and service that was needed. I also received a loan of *eleven*

hundred dollars. I placed a down payment on an apartment and

furniture. While my car was being fixed, my supervisor and I drove

down to Virginia to pick my kids up.

I had to move out of the barracks. I spent most of the days

that were left on the pass to move my items into the apartment.

My car was fixed, and I could get around much better. My commander had surprised me by giving me a waiver for promotion to Specialist. I really needed all the extra money that I could get. I was so thankful to have such wonderful supervisors and co-workers and a wonderful commander. I was happy to have people like them in my corner. I had to enroll the children in daycare. Luckily, the daycare was priced by household income.

In the midst of all of the chaos, I'd forgotten about Jeremy. He contacted me to ask me how I was doing. I told him that I was doing fine. I invited him over to my empty apartment and he came over. I hadn't gotten my furniture delivered, yet. He met my kids and began to come over more often. I guess he enjoyed coming over a lot. We'd been together for about four months, when I became disturbed by the fact that Jeremy had pictures of his ex-bitches still hanging on his wall, in the barracks. I told him that I didn't feel comfortable with them up. I asked him to take them down and he did. I noticed that he was always on IM. I kind of blew that off. I had been hurt too many times before, and I refused to go through it anymore. I also asked him to take down the posters of the naked females that were hanging on the walls. He ignored me. One day, I came by his room and he was on the phone. He was answering the person's questions with one word answers. I couldn't believe he thought that I was that naïve and stupid. If it's one thing that I can't stand, it's a cheater. I told him beforehand that if he wanted someone else, then he should move on and not cheat on me. He would get more respect in doing that than thinking he was going to play me. I also noticed that he still had the posters of the naked bitches up. I became furious, and I barged in his room and ripped them all down. Jeremy kept on persisting to try his luck at making me angry. When I'd come over, he'd try to hurry up and log off of IM. I knew the bastard was up to something. I just couldn't put my finger on it. I guess he didn't have enough balls to break up with me. He would do things to try to make me mad, so that I would break up with him. Little did he know, he was in this for the long haul. I decided that I wasn't going to be one that slept around. I was going to make us work, whether he liked it or not. If he wanted out of the relationship, I wasn't going to make it easy for his dumb ass. He tried, on many occasions, to break our relationship off, but I wasn't having that. He stopped coming over and he started hanging out with his friends. He knew that I couldn't get out because of the kids. He would use that to his advantage. One night, I decided to pop-up on him at his barracks room. I was hoping to catch him with a bitch so that I'd have an excuse to whoop his ass and her's, too. I had built up anger and aggression that I didn't know was bottled inside of me. That night, Jeremy brought it out of me. We had a disagreement, and we began to argue. Then, it happened. He said something that was over the line, and I commenced to putting my hands on him.

I asked him, "Are you thinking of replacing me?"

He responded, "You're already replaced. Ha ha!"

I didn't like that comment at all. He just so happened to be leaning back in his chair when he made the comment. I stood up and over him, and I pushed him down to the floor. I guess he felt stupid. He jumped up and started pushing me towards the door, telling me to get out of his room. I kept telling him that I didn't have to go anywhere. He kept grabbing my arm really tight, and I told him to let my arm go. He wouldn't do it. So, I ripped his shirt right off of his body. He was shocked. The more he pushed me towards the door, the more I pushed him in the opposite direction. He'd met his match. I wanted to fuck him up so badly. I told him to fuck off, and I left. The next day, at work, Jeremy made it his business to come and bother me. He was trying to crack jokes to make me smile, but I wasn't having it. That pussy had the audacity to tell me that I was replaced and then act like he didn't say that. He tried to tell me that he was just kidding. I blew him off. He told me that he'd never met a female that crossed the line of putting their hands on him. I told him that I wasn't an average bitch that took anybody's shit. At that point in my life, I was too tired of bullshit. We ended up making up, and I forgave him for the comment that he made.

A month had passed, and I found myself always arguing with Jeremy. He was getting on my nerves, but I didn't want to start all over with someone else. It was the month of July, and our unit was going on summer break. I'd been putting up with Jeremy's bullshit for so long, that it was second nature. One day, I decided to visit him, and he wanted to break it off with me. I told him that we weren't breaking up. He kept on insisting, and I was going to give in, until we walked into the hallway. Some bitch was walking, and he screamed out her name. I asked him how he knew the bitch. He just laughed and went towards her daughter, with open arms, so he could hug her. I told him that if he hugged that little bitch, he was going to regret every minute of his life. He chose not to hug the child. He tried to introduce me to the bitch and her fat ass friend, but I ignored them and kept on yelling at him. I kept yelling that he was a lying, cheating faggot. I yelled at him for another *thirty* minutes. Jeremy had threatened to call the Staff

Duty personnel to have me escorted out of the barracks. Since I

had my children and I had to move out of the barracks, I really

didn't have any business being there. My mother had my children

for the summer, and I was going to use my summer break to go

and get them from Virginia. No one, in my unit, liked Jeremy. They

told me, numerous times, to get rid of him. All he did was stress

me out with all of his lying and cheating. I just wouldn't let it go.

The Staff Duty supervisor finally arrived, and he just so happened

to be one of the supervisors in my platoon. He told me to step

away from Jeremy's door, and I told him that he could close the

door whenever the hell he wanted to. I also told him that I was

doing no harm by standing in the hallway and no one owned the

hallway. It was a free country. Jeremy proceeded to close the

door in my face. I wasn't having that bullshit. I kicked his door

back open and told him that if he closed the door in my face, I was

going to kill him. The Staff Duty supervisor grabbed me by the arm

and began to reason with me. He told me that Jeremy didn't

deserve me and he was worthless. He told me to walk with him. I was crying, frantically. I wanted to kill that bastard. I wouldn't budge. I screamed, out loud, that I was going to kill myself. The supervisor grabbed my arm and pulled me to walk down the hall to talk to him. He told me that because I said that phrase, he couldn't allow me to go home by myself. I told him that I was okay. He walked me to his car. We got in it and drove to my car, which was around the corner. He talked to me for about *forty* minutes. I got in my car and I left to go home. I was so hurt that I kept contemplating on ending my life. I figured that it was never meant for me to be happy, at all. I'd come to the conclusion that I was going to be lonely for the rest of my life, and I wanted my life to end. I wanted everyone around me to be hurt. I thought that people would miss me when I wasn't around. I felt under appreciated by others. I didn't care about anything, anymore. I thought that I was supposed to be cheated on, beat on, and lied to by all men that come into my life. My heart was sore, and I wanted it all to end. I did the only thing that I knew how to do. I grabbed a bottle of pills and turned it up to my mouth. After I'd taken the pills, my phone rang. It was Jeremy. I asked him what he wanted.

He asked, "You're not really going to kill yourself, are you?"

I said, "It's too late to act like you care. Besides, I already took some pills."

I hung up and went to take a shower. I just wanted to lie down and go to sleep, forever. *Fifteen* minutes passed and the phone rang, again. It was Jeremy. I didn't catch on, at first, but he asked me what my address was. I gave him the first three numbers of my address, and I had second thoughts. I told him to fuck off, and I hung up the phone. I sat on the couch and began to doze off, until I heard some sirens. I thought nothing of it, but the sound wasn't fading. The sound seemed to get closer and closer to my neighborhood. There was a knock at the door. I opened it, groggy and all. It was a female State Trooper. She'd explained that she received a call about a suicide attempt and she wanted to come in. I let her in and told her that there was no such thing going on. She'd received the information from the Military Police. Apparently, Jeremy called the Military Police to tell them about my suicide attempt. There was only one problem. I lived off post and they had no jurisdiction. They called the Staff Duty personnel and demanded that the chain of command be notified of the incident. The Military Police contacted the State Patrol personnel. Two EMT crews arrived shortly after the State Trooper. I was very pissed. The trooper asked me if she could see the bottle that I had taken the pills from. I told her that I didn't take that many pills. She insisted that she see the bottle. I retrieved the bottle from the trash can, and she inspected it. Meanwhile, the EMT crew checked my vitals and my pupils. I told them that I didn't take that many pills, and I knew how many pills to take before there was severe damage to my body. The crew deemed that I was fine and my vitals were normal. The Trooper, being a soft ass female, still wanted me to seek mental help from a professional. I told her that I was fine, but she just wasn't having that. My supervisor arrived, and the trooper told him to take me to the hospital for urgent care, immediately. She said that she was going to call the hospital later on and check if I did. I got dressed, and my supervisor drove me to the hospital. When I arrived at the hospital, I asked to speak to a mental health doctor. I was told to fill out some paperwork and have a seat. My commander, my supervisor, his supervisor, and a few people from my platoon had shown up. I couldn't believe the support that I had gotten. I didn't mean for all of that to happen. I didn't want everyone to have to stop what they were doing to tend to me. I was sort of embarrassed. They were all very supportive.

After hours of being in the emergency area and hours of being lied to, the on-call doctor decided to admit me into the psych ward. I didn't want to go. My commander told them to explain why they were prolonging my stay and telling us that I could go home that night but showing no effort in letting me go. No one had an explanation. My commander told me that I was going to be okay and she would come and see me in the morning.

She told me to cooperate with the hospital personnel. I wanted to fight the world. I was enraged. I wanted to kill everyone that ever lied to me and did me wrong. The first day that I was on the ward, the doctor called me into his office. He wanted to interview me. I asked him when I was leaving. He told me that since it was the weekend, he could not discharge me. Once again, a lie that caught up to me. I wanted to cry. I didn't eat or leave my room all day long. One of the nurses, that had to give progress reports, came into my room and explained to me that everything that I did or didn't do was being documented. It wasn't helping that I wasn't eating. I was really showing signs of depression. The second day, I attended the required group meetings. I'd remembered the code of one of my calling cards, so I used it to call Jeremy. That bastard. He admitted to calling the authorities on me because he was concerned. I reminded him of his not wanting to be with me anymore. He apologized to me and told me that he would visit me. Later on, it was found to be a lie. I should've known better. *Four* days later, I was released. I couldn't believe that I was on a psych ward for taking some damn aspirin. I was on a ward with people who'd tried to drown themselves, slit their wrists, hang themselves, and much worse stuff. I was happy to get out of there. I just wanted to go and get my kids.

I arrived in Virginia a few days after that mishap. My mother tried talking my head off about the situation, but I didn't want to hear that bullshit. I called Jeremy, at his mother's house, in New Jersey. I asked him what happened to his visiting me. He told me that he just couldn't see me in that condition and he felt bad that it was his fault that I was there. He told me that he'd come down to visit me at my mother's house. He did. Jeremy began to say all kinds of bullshit about him wanting to still be with me and I was a cool person. He just couldn't take my anger and my putting my hands on him. He said that I was abusive. What do some people expect when they lie and cheat on a person? Some people get caught up in unbelievable circumstances and they don't know how to handle them.

CHAPTER FOURTEEN-REALIZING MY PURPOSE

The relationship between me and Jeremy was on and off. We would break up and make up many times. It became our routine. I found out that he had cheated on me with some white chick during one of our break ups. Though we had many break ups, I hadn't slept with anyone else. I was hurt and disgusted when I found that out. That was the last straw. I told him that I was done with him. He didn't believe me. I had gone through telling him that I loved him and him telling me that he loved me to him taking it back. He said that he was drunk when he told me that he loved me. He said that he was taking back what he had said. That was the dumbest thing I had ever heard from anyone. We had spent the next few months arguing about his cheating and lying. I had gotten so fed up with his bullshit. I went to his room to tell him that it was over between us. On the way, I had changed my mind. I was just going to talk to him to see where his head was at. He ended up telling me that he wanted someone else and he was tired of arguing. I told him when I walked out the door I was not coming back. He told me that he didn't care. I asked him if he was sure that he meant that. He told me that he did, and I left. I didn't look back. It was kind of a breath of fresh air. I no longer had to worry about someone lying to me or cheating on me. I was free. My heart was hurt, at first, but I got over him. The New Year had come, and I started dating someone else. He was sweet and he paid attention to everything that I said and did. Unfortunately, I had been so used to being treated like shit, that I didn't know what it was to be treated like a lady. I had to let that guy go. We remain friends to this day. My heart wasn't truly emptied out from being with Jeremy. I decided to try to be to myself. I needed to see and feel what that was like. I needed to get to know *me*, for a change. One day, I decided to call my children's father. I needed help with my youngest son's daycare bill. He wasn't in school, yet, and the bill was *one hundred ninety* dollars per month. With all of the bills that I had, it was becoming harder for me to survive as a single parent. I asked Zic if he could help me out and send me *two hundred* dollars a month to help out with our youngest son's daycare bill.

He said, "Fuck you and fuck helping the kids. I don't think he's mine, anyway."

He hung up. I didn't deserve that. He was living free, and I was stuck with the kids. The following week, I decided to go to the social services office to receive assistance. I was told that I made too much money. The worker asked me if the father was supporting the children. I told her that I wasn't. The worker gathered all of Zic's information from me and processed the paperwork. She told me that she was going to have him summoned for a DNA test and child support. She told me that I shouldn't have to go through raising children alone. The day came for us to take the swab tests. Zic was in a Virginia paternity office, and at the same time, the kids and I were in a New York paternity office. We had to wait two weeks for the results. I hadn't noticed that it was taking a little longer than what was told to me. I received a phone call at *one* in the morning. It was my mother.

The bitch didn't even say hello.

She said, "Is there something you need to tell me?"

I didn't have a clue what she was talking about. She was pissing me off.

I said, "No."

She told me that she received the DNA test results, and Zic was not the father of my oldest son. It really wasn't too much of a shock to me. The results were accidentally sent to her address, because of her receiving prior assistance from the state. It was always in the back of my mind that Zic wasn't my oldest son's father. That was something that was pushed aside during all the years. Two weeks before I'd met Zic, I had sex with a guy that I went to high school with. We were unprotected, and in the middle of sex, he had asked me if he could come in me. I told him not to, and I pushed him off of me. I kicked him out of my house and didn't speak to him, again. My mother asked me if I knew who the father was. I told her that I did and it was none of her business. I hung up the phone, in shock. Zic called me a couple of days later. He tried to act hurt. I told him that I wasn't going to let him disown his child, because he was there when he was born. I also told him that it would've been different if he was a real father to the children. All he cared about was himself. I told him to never call me again. I told him that we were maintaining just fine without him or anyone else. I hung up the phone and I went on about my business.

I ended up getting back with Jeremy, and he went to another duty station. We agreed that I would reenlist to get stationed where he was going. I had to wait for *nine* months before I was able to reenlist. It was later brought to me that I could reenlist early to go to one of three duty stations. One of the choices happened to be where Jeremy was. I reenlisted and called Jeremy to tell him the news. He pretended to be happy. I was really raining on his cheating parade. I decided to check something that came to my mind one night. I typed in Jeremy's user name on a website and took a stab at guessing his password. The password

that dawned on me was the password that got me into all of his

accounts. That man had been cheating on me since the day we'd

met. I was furious. I logged onto his IM and pretended to be him,

online. I told all of the bitches that he had a wife and he was just

using them for money and sex. I guess he was getting a lot of

phone calls, so he called me and asked if I was going into his

accounts. I told him that I was woman about what I did. I told him

that I was, in fact, going into his accounts. I told him that I was

going to whoop his ass when I got down to Georgia. I knew he was

shook. He played hard but was a soft pussy.

Time flew by rather quickly. I arrived in Georgia. It was the

summer time, and it was hot as hell. That meant that I had to

dress in less clothing. When Jeremy saw me with skimpy shorts

on, he tried to walk behind me so that no one could look at my

butt. He was jealous and it was funny as hell. The tables were

slowly turning, and I was pleased. I was finally getting a taste of real, black men. There weren't that many to choose from in New York. I had a well-rounded pick. I still remained faithful, even though that sucker deserved to be treated like he had treated me. Once again, I began catching him in lies. He was still seeing other females. I had found all of his ex-bitches' pictures, and I destroyed them all. I destroyed every letter that he had saved from those bitches.

Our units were set to deploy to Iraq very soon, and we were going to be apart for a year. I thought that I wouldn't be able to handle that. Jeremy's unit left first, and I was sad. I cried the whole day. I soon got over it, though. That was my chance to get back at him. I ended up conversing with someone who was interested in me. I later decided to take it a step further with the guy. My unit left a couple of days later. Jeremy and I found out that we were going to be in the same area for a few days. We hooked up and he started buying me everything that I wanted. He even did something that he had never done before. He bought me a card. I was in shock. He told me that he had a bad dream that I was cheating on him. He told me that he was sorry for everything that he'd done to me. I just sat there and listened. I even felt kind of guilty for cheating on him, but he brought it on himself. With all of the shit that he had done to me, it was bound to happen.

The next day, his unit left. A few days later, my unit left to head to our set place of deployment. Our units ended up being an hour and a half away from each other. That time had given me a chance to think. I needed to re-evaluate my life and its priorities. I was heading down the road to destruction and it wasn't pretty. One day, I decided to sit down and write a list of all of my priorities. One of my priorities was to pay off everything that was on my credit report. I wrote my own payment plan, and within four months, I paid my credit off. The babysitter that I had found, in Georgia, was keeping my children while I was deployed. I only had to pay her what I could afford. That worked out for me, perfectly. My own mother wanted *twelve hundred* dollars a month for keeping my children. I am glad that my babysitter agreed to care of them while I was gone. As the months went on

in Iraq, I learned more and more about myself. I decided that I

had a lot to offer the world. God has blessed me with many

talents and I shouldn't let them go to waste. I had to live for

myself and for my children. I wanted to make my children proud

of me. I wanted them to have someone that they could look up to

and admire. I am happy to report that the mission is accomplished

and I have realized my purpose—that's to guard the soul, that was

once stolen, and take care of it with all of my might.

About the Author

Kelichia decided to write the story of her early life. Everyone who has come into contact with her has always been interested in what gives her the drive that she constantly has. In hearing all that she has gone through, she was told that she should allow people to hear her story all over the world. She wants to give people an idea of where she comes from as a person. She wants to inspire anyone who is going through hard situations. She enjoys every bit of her life and is grateful for everything and everyone that has come into her life. The

situations that are mentioned in The Men That Stole My Soul are

a few of the many that she has gone through. She hopes that this

book touches the lives and souls of everyone that reads it.